STREAMS

STREAMS

Life-Secrets for Writing Poems and Songs

by

Sandra Hochman

Foreword by

Galt MacDermot
composer of "Hair"

TURNER

Turner Publishing Company
Nashville, Tennessee
New York, New York
www.turnerpublishing.com

Streams: Life Secrets for Writing Poems and Songs

Cover design:
Book design: Glen M. Edelstein

Library of Congress Cataloging-in-Publication Data
Names: Hochman, Sandra, author.
Title: Streams : life-secrets for writing poems and songs / by Sandra Hochman.
Description: Nashville, Tennessee : Turner Publishing Company, [2017]
Identifiers: LCCN 2017002569 | ISBN 9781683365310 (pbk. : alk. paper)
Subjects: LCSH: Poetics. | Poetry--Authorship. | Popular music--Writing and
 publishing.
Classification: LCC PN1042 .H55 2017 | DDC 808.1--dc23
LC record available at https://lccn.loc.gov/2017002569

9781683365310

Printed in the United States of America
17 18 19 20 10 9 8 7 6 5 4 3 2 1

Rhythm and timing are everything to a poet.
I have used my own life to forge out my songs.
I dedicate this book to writers who, with joy and desperation,
cast their lives into their work.

I also dedicate this book to Robert Stewart,
who made this book come into my mind;
to Ariel, my daughter, a young poet;
to Marita, who created an evening of my work;
to Teddy, who helps me teach children to bring
their lives to writing.

Contents

FOREWORD by Galt MacDermot   ix

INTRODUCTION   1

CHAPTER ONE   The Opening of the Mind   7

CHAPTER TWO   Words   31

CHAPTER THREE   Subjects for Poems   61

CHAPTER FOUR   Writing Songs   139

Foreword

by Galt MacDermot, composer of *Hair*

THE ART OF WRITING SONGS for me, as a composer, is not a matter of collaboration. That comes later with the singing, staging, or general selling that is involved in today's setup. The actual work of composing music goes on in one head at a time, and ideally it will happen after a poet has gone through his or her own process of composing the poem. Which brings us to the subject of this book—the poet.

My experience with poetry is that it is the perfect inspiration for melody. There are others, like plain elation or gloominess or a dramatic situation. But for that clear unfolding, seemingly on its own, of a stream of delightful notes clustering around a beautiful rhythm, there is nothing like a page or so of works willed into place by a poet.

What makes one person a poet and another not is a mystery. In my school days of learning to compose I used to search through poetry anthologies. I suppose because they were all in there, they were all poets, but some made music and some just didn't. There is a sort of perfume that a poem exudes that triggers something in the brain that starts to jiggle the words around into something that if you catch it, can be a song.

Sandra Hochman is one of those people who put words together in such a way that when you read them you hear them with that extra part of your mind that deals with something other than information; in other words, she is a poet. Because she is also somewhat of an intellectual, a liberated woman, and a business genius, she writes very differently from anyone I've worked with before and that is refreshing, but the real test of why you write with a person is not what they write about, but what their writing does when it goes into the candy-floss machine in the upper reaches of your mind. Does it start the wheels turning? Sandra's does.

STREAMS

Introduction

THIS IS A PERSONAL BOOK that I hope will be like a friend. In a simple way I want to tell you some thoughts that I have about writing poetry and songs, and share with you some warm-up exercises for writing that can be used to limber up the mind the same way that dancers limber before a performance. Writing has always been for me a necessary experience—something that I feel compelled to do. If that feeling of wanting to write is inside of you—what I call the Necessary Angel wanting to speak—that writing can be a part of your life experience the way it is part of mine.

The book that is here is put together in a nonconventional way. Like the *Book of Changes,* you should be able to open it at any point and find some thought that can spark your own imagination. Since writing is a lonely art, think of this book as a friend whose encouragement can lead you into your own mind.

Nobody can tell anyone how to write. Writing often comes out of very mysterious sources. But I do believe that we can all be helped by learning from the experience of others. These thoughts or life-secrets may lead you to have the confidence to go deep down into your own writing self.

Finally, to me, writing is a way of entering. It is something that requires practice and almost daily renewal. It is an art that is never mastered but can give great challenge to the person writing. In the end, one is always one's own critic, one's own master, and no one can take that individual responsibility out of writing. It is a way of finally being alone with your own thoughts, fantasies, and angers, and making something the way a potter makes a pot.

In the Empty Room of Perfection

Love
Opened my eyes to the amulets
of trees—
Green leaves, falling miracles,
Falling, one by one,
On the street. In Japan we bought

White porcelain tipped into palm-eyes
And icicles, pots shaped like
Peach stones and glazed in sky blue.
We touched the rims of the world's glaze
But arrived without anything. Then
You gave me my own room without old things,
Without decorations, without paintings
That hang on the walls
Only to become new walls themselves, without
Shapes that interfere
With what I must be.

My dreams were unshaped and unpainted. I
Lived with the fantasy of the sea—shaped
Always on the verge of words. You—
Looked for emptiness the way lovers seek sleep,
Burned currencies
And seeds of your own beginnings. How easy
For us to change into firebirds, fly
Past history, oceans, striking against the sky

With our own new wings. Now—
Shall we return where we came from?
You be the brush that strikes.
And, burning inside, still burning, I'll
Live as the flaming kiln that shapes the pot.

To me writing is learning how not to be afraid, how to open doors, how to imagine accidents on paper—learning how to be open to language. Open to experience. Open to nature, to faces, to the senses. Most of all open to one's own inner life. I really feel that I have been encouraged, that certain people have passed on to me their secrets. As a child, I learned from books. Later still, I met many artists. I met Camus. And Neruda. And Lowell. And Bellow. I met Elizabeth Bishop. And T. S. Eliot. And Sartre. I met composers that I learned from—Stravinsky, Shostakovich. I met writers who encouraged me—Anaïs Nin, who taught me that writing is a generosity of the spirit, that involvement in the art of letters is the art of jousting with energy, loving others, and giving away all of oneself to others—in the celebration of life. It was Anaïs who, in Paris, published my first book of poems with Lawrence Durrell—oddly enough without ever having read a poem that I had written. "I know that you are a poet," she said. "I can tell. And poets need their work published."

What made me a writer? My mother taking me to museums. Apple trees that I dreamed under. Songs that I learned. Girls in boarding school. Women in college. Old people that told me about their lives. Stranger after stranger and lover after lover. The Hudson River. Miami palm trees. Stones in Ossining. Fears in boarding school. Geraniums. Cats. Butterflies and moths. Streets in Paris. Odd people I slept with. The words in dictionaries. The words on the tongues of strangers. All of these people and places taught me to write.

Learning to fly a plane, learning to play tennis, learning to jog, learning t'ai chi ch'uan, learning to laugh, to sit in silence in the Sangenjaya gardens, learning to listen, to make a fool of myself, to give birth, to hang up the phone when necessary—all of these things have taught me about writing poetry. But none of them has taught me. I write because I have to write. I want to write. I love, perhaps am even obsessed with, the sounds and rhythms of words. For me this is a way of living. I know of no other way to make myself happy.

When did you begin writing?

People ask me that.

All that I know about poetry is locked up in my poems. I have written:

All that I wanted
When I once wanted everything
Was this
To be allowed to name things. To discover,
Like Noah, the name of each vegetable,
To discover each word as if I had invented it.

I learned about poetry by listening to music. My mother sent me at the age of four to the Master Institute, which was a large brick building on Riverside Drive. To make music. To dance to music. Music and dance. Four years old. That was my first lesson. Dancing. Clapping my hands. Making my body move. My ears listen. Lessons in rhythms. I still believe that poetry is music. That poetry and rhythms are all tied up.

When did you start writing? I was writing in my crib. I was making a dream log. I was wishing things different. As I stood in my crib and cried and looked out at the Hudson shining its colors in the sun, I was already evoking dreams, listening to arguments, creating new dialogues for those who came through the house. I was writing in my head. Which is, I think, where all writing begins. In the iris of the eye. In the tympanum of the ear. In the map of the line longing to be a lifeline that can touch everything. In the spying on elders. Remembering conversations. Remembering dreams. Operating on owlish levels that no one understands, especially the owl. Swimming in words. Looking at colors. Catching the colors of the Hudson. *It all begins in what you hear. What you see.* In my crib, in my lonely crib, I was writing even then.

Wonder

Two worlds stared at each other for some time,
Then, in a flash, collided. It was dark
But luckily it happened near a park.
Two worlds fell on the branches of one tree.

The east of distance west of what is near——
O apple that we long to touch and hear
Oil-painted mauve, a foreign mystery
This real unreal still poised upon a tree.

But those who are born blind, or have not heard
About the famed macabre clash of words
Still listen with an ear bent toward the moon,
And wonder if it might fall on their mouth.

CHAPTER ONE

The Opening
of
the Mind

WE CAN ALL SAY THAT WE HAVE different histories or different parts of us that could be autobiographied. Just as a doctor takes your "medical history"—little questionnaires ask, "Have you ever had measles, chicken pox? When did you have your first operation?"—we could make up similar imaginative histories for different parts of our lives. Our cooking histories would be different from our political histories. And yet as I try to isolate my writing history there are certain events that I could name that have been important to me in my life as a writer.

To begin with, no one starts life as a "writer."

I was a child who dreamed of being a great tapdancer or comedian or actress. My mother took me to a lot of museums in New York City, and I began, even as a child, to know that there was "life" and there was "art." Art was plays. Art was music. Art was paintings. Art was books. Art was the sculpture that I saw in museums. Like all children I was an artist too, but I didn't know it. Nobody told me I was an artist. That was something I had to tell myself many years later. Artists, by the way—particularly poets—only become artists by naming themselves. You are the first person who pronounces yourself a poet or artist or songwriter. *You bless yourself, create yourself, name yourself, and think of yourself as a writer, and as you do that you become one.* You don't have to go to a graduate school—you are your own graduate school. You give yourself your own profession by simply saying, "This is what I am."

I remember writing at the age of seven. By that time I was already reading a lot of books and making up my own songs and stories in my head. I was dreaming, imagining, storytelling, rhyming, singing, dancing, and creating another world than the one I lived in. Nobody cared. That was part of the wonder of it all. I cared. It all began with solitude, loneliness, and imagination. Reading. And thinking up ways to escape my childhood, which I hated.

I hated being powerless.

I hated being an only child.

I hated having no one to talk to during the boring long afternoons of being seven.

By seven I was in the second grade. I had already gone to several different schools. Since my mother was a teacher, she was crazy about education. By the time I was seven I was practically a doctoral candidate. I had gone to pre-prekindergarten, where I learned how to make snakes out of clay, and prekindergarten, where I learned to fingerpaint and dance. I had taken piano lessons and many other lessons in kindergarten at Fieldston in Riverdale (we had moved from New York City to the country of Riverdale). I had learned how to read and by the time I was in the first grade I was reading all the time. Between the first grade and the second grade my parents separated and that's when I think I began writing in my head. I didn't call it writing. I didn't call "It" anything. But what I was doing was writing poems.

> Give up perfection now and learn to call
> Old sounds false, and true sounds beautiful.
> We are the summit of the hills we see.
> Two wings of sunset beat inside our minds
> And we become the sunset and the sun.
> Also, pine trees, bending in the earth
> Like dancers tipped upon a stage,
> Become the silent dancers who are part
> Of everything we listened for and thought.
> We are the summit of the hills we see—
> Matrix of that falcon sun and all
> Things renewed inside the eye's whirl.

Writing is a way of expressing thought and feeling and observances. It is also a way of getting away from "real life" and inventing a symbolic world that exists through the symbol of words. The discipline of writing, then, is a discipline of thought. It is a way of getting rid of thought onto paper—of capturing thought through words.

If writing is to be understood at all, it is, in my opinion, a personal voice in the distance. It is energy. It is life. It is who we are.

I think you can teach people how to write—by showing them a way to unlock themselves. I have taught at universities, private schools, and have been going down, down to children—finally founding a school of my own (location: the Metropolitan Museum of Art in New York City) to open the doors of experience for children. The school is called You're an Artist Too. There are no classrooms—just the open classroom for twenty young poets to wander around, look at art, listen to guest speakers, and be given exercises to write. In a sense one can only create the "atmosphere" for young people or people of any age to magically open up to themselves. By getting young people to tell how they think about themselves, how to look at their own bodies, hands, feet—how to examine their feelings and not be ashamed to put on paper what they imagine. This is part of "writing." It is not "learning" to write—it is being "who you are." In this sense confessional writing tells a lot. "Getting it out" is part of "going beyond" the self into writing.

Almost everyone I know or that I meet has thought of writing. It is as if a "life story" is locked inside everyone. I met a tennis teacher who had worked for two years at the Club Méditerranée at Guadeloupe. He told me, "I want to write the exposé of Club Méd. I was there for two years. I can write it from the inside and make millions of dollars. If you want to write it for me I'll give you a fifty-fifty split." If I said to this uneducated tycoon-of-the-imagination that I was going to play at Wimbledon, he'd say, "Never. You can't play professional tennis."

This man only dreams of paperback sales and movies. This is why there are so many "potential authors" and not enough people who view writing, like tennis, as a way of life. If this man had realized that the thousands of hours he spent perfecting his stroke, or serve, or running, or backhand were what made him able to play tennis—that the years of training of perfecting his body as his instrument is no different from what a "writer" does—he would have understood that the athletic life—the life of persons perfecting themselves for better health or accuracy—or even to compete against others in skill—is not unlike a metaphor for the writing. *Writing, like tennis, is a way of living one's life.* Just as "Zen" tennis is a technique of hitting the ball and becoming in harmony with the ball or "Zen" archery is a way of hitting the center of a target but at the same time "centering" on the self, "Zen" writing might be writing as a way of transcending the real life and entering into another sphere. Centering on the inner life and turning it to song.

If poetry is health, words are a key to this health.

Accuracy of observation is the equivalent of accuracy of thinking.
Lists are ideas.
There is no accuracy of thinking without accuracy of words. A poet is always spying on new vocabularies.

Wallace Stevens has written: "In poetry you must love the words, the ideas, the images and rhythms with all your capacity to love anything at all." Sentimentality is often not a failure of feeling, but a failure of finding the right words. We live in the mind—but we write in the mind transposed by words.

Yeats talks about creating a poem "fit to live in." Words are the bricks for the imaginary house.

Poems are new sounds. They have rhythms which soothe us, and they are the means of expressing ideas. Once there was sound. The sound of people waking up to life. Perhaps the sound of animals and people was one. The animal sound was there before there were people. Sounds made by insects and reptiles and prehistoric animals. These primitive sounds are lost to us. (The Eohippus had no recording company.) But through the study of primitive people today we can imagine how the earliest tribes spoke. And the first words that they had were words for nature—darkness and light—words for the newness of things. Words were the way to reveal the world—from one person to another. A form of silence that became sound.

If one imagines what the earliest sounds (pre words) used by people were, one must think of monosyllabic sounds. The Chinese language, which is one of the earliest languages, even to the moment is based on one word/one sound—it is monosyllabic. Which leads one to believe that the earliest words were simple sounds. Chinese characters suggest that the earliest words that were written were pictograms—drawings of an object, scene. Take the word for horse—the original Chinese character looked like this:

The modern Chinese word still keeps its resemblance and looks like this:

Also, sound of that word in Chinese is like a horse neighing: maaaaaaaa. In Chinese, words are conceived of as being exact. In Chinese we have the basis of poetry in the ideogram (idea-o-gram)—the idea close to the pictorial form.

EXERCISE: Write about ordinary things. Write about a broom, or a teacup, or any ordinary object. Find words that *sound* like what they are. Whoosh of water. Plop of a mop. Blimpy words that are fat, crash words. Don't be afraid of being childish or of the essential craziness of hearing things for the first time.

Just as Kafka kept notebooks of dreams, the poet can keep notebooks of words. Words are dreams which the poet puts consciously together.

Victor Rosen, M.D., notes that a child's first sounds are babbling—at which time the extremities, particularly the arms, join in a mimetic-gestural system in which a "complex eshema [exercise] for signalling becomes integrated with the vocal sound." Babbling becomes language.

Everything that the poet Wallace Stevens wrote was related to how he wrote poetry. His idea was involved with the concept of the ordinary man, a man "master of himself" as the hero—not the extraordinary "monster." In the poems he persists "like the prismatic formations that occur about us in nature in the case of reflections and refractions."

> Ariel was glad he had written his poems.
> They were of a remembered time
> Or of something seen that he had liked.

Wallace Stevens also said, "The World of The Poet depends on the world that he has contemplated." Let us leave, for a moment, the world of commercial contemplations. Let us think of words as not a way of "selling," but a way of expressing "being." For me poems often come out imaginary letters to someone.

EXERCISE: Write an imaginary letter to someone.

Heroes

> I think of the anguish of slaves
> And open my veins. Buy carnations
> And drink canned nectar. It is absurd
> To look for you in the
> Marriage bed. You're on a Greyhound
> Bus riding away.

I write to you
Thinking of the way you combed your hair
Over the sink. To you—practicing
The fiddle in the dark,
Driving down highways
In your banged-up car. Gods are the loneliest
Men. And heroes make their
Women slaves.

Ladder of love,
Hold me now.
Climbing on bare feet,
Hold me now.
Women can no longer love. Hold
On tight. I am writing
This letter without
A pencil.

It is too dark here to tell you
What I was saying—
You will soon be

South. It's dark in my city. Such
Evidence is little to build on. But
It is all I have.

Writing poetry is a way of trying to commune with others—giving them, the others, a way of dazzling and accelerating their own life-beat. By opening up to "oneself" one opens to others. Not to be afraid of one's own life, childhood, separations. Everything is a subject for poetry. When I gave birth to my daughter, I imagined trying to open my mind to the experience of the body. I saw birth as a subject for poems:

The First Meeting

I shall meet you at
The instant of your birth
When you emerge from the red leaves,
Dripping from the seashells in my skin.

You have been swimming, too,
Against the salt weeds
Under the red leaves.

Then I shall meet you,
See you, and tell you how many mornings
Of my life

I have been sleeping
Under the flame trees,
My veins splayed

Like the veins of leaves
Reaching beyond me
And caught in the air.

For I have always
Wanted to be born, to be
Reborn each morning.

And in your beginning

I find my own meaning.

What shall I say, what
Shall I tell you
When I meet you
For the first time?

Opening oneself up to all experiences is the essence of writing. Tapping that deep feeling and not being afraid to say what you feel. For me, even a car accident and being stranded—a mundane subject—is a subject for a poem. Delmore Schwartz taught me to write about drugstores, supermarkets. Marianne Moore taught me to really look at unimportant things and see deep inside of them for the poem. The opening of the mind to all experience is really finding the poet inside of you. Here is an example of a poem about an accident.

Poem for Alexandra

When idiots ask me, "How do you write your poems?"
I'll tell them, "Pink shells. Pink shells." You
Will know what I mean. Think

Of the afternoon
When the gulls wheeled over the garbage of Three Mile Harbor
And the car, my gray Valiant, was suddenly curved
into sand. Think of us all getting out, watching it sag
Into the sand. It was only a mimic accident
But it kept us from going where we were going. As
The farm boy who came by to help ran home for his rope
I felt helpless and impatient
Because accidents are always a long waste
Of time. And I felt wrong

Leaving you staring at the car—the helpless car
Sinking like a compact gray steel whale—
But there was nothing I could do so I walked away
Down the road to look at the sea flay the rocks gently. And I think
I went to pray.
Not for the car, certainly, but to give praise
For our afternoon which had been warm, perfect as a gift.
It was then—as the farm boys were yanking the car
Out of the sand—
That I saw the shells, the amazing twisting shells,

Spirals pink, rose, calcified sea bones,
Shells in splayed conches, strange, beaten apart
By waves so that their hearts, that part that curves
And forms a peeling shelter of its own,
Were proud hosannas carved from the breathing water
And tossed to me by the wind.
I worked fast. There was not much time
Before the car was towed out of the sand. And I picked

Them quickly. I didn't want to waste a second
And gathered as many shells as my arms could hold.
I brought them back to the scene of the accident
Feeling ridiculous.
I'd been busy with seashells instead of observing the car.
But calamities and minor accidents

Give us time to discover what is around us.
We got back in the car. As we drove by the wall of the sea
Remember that I told you that ridiculous stops
Are always turned to advantage—in improbable times
We discover whatever mystery we can. So whenever they
Want answers about the invisible
I'll tell them, "Pink shells. The pink shells," and

Think of the accident, Alexandra,
Think of the pink shells!

EXERCISE: Write a poem about an experience you have had that was an accident.

Poems can be short histories of events. A little Decline and Fall of a Relationship, your own version of *The Decline and Fall of the Roman Empire*. This "history" of feelings is in my poem "The Couple."

The Couple

A Greek ship
Sails on the sea

Carrying me past
The islands
Into an unknown
Island where
The burros
Are sleeping, houses
Are white, and brown
Honey is sold in
The general store. That's
Me up on the hill,
Living with the
Man I'm going
To marry. There
We are. He plays
The violin
But never practices—
I fold and unfold
The nylon blouses
I brought from
America and put
Them neatly in
A drawer. It's
Time to go out.
We explore the island
And at the same time
Argue about
Getting married.
We walk close to
The sea, which happens
To knock our eyes
Out with its blue. An
Old lady, call her a
Witch, passes us by and
Asks us the way to
The post office.

We continue on the rocks,
Walking by the sea. "I bet
We look married," I say,
And turn my eyes from
The sea. "Only to
An old lady going
To mail
Letters at the post
Office," you reply.
And begin to weep. Not
One snorkel——
That will float
Us under the sea
To schools of fish
Who are enjoying
Their mateless
Existence——will
Take us away from
Our troubles. The
Young girl folds
Up her blouses and
Begins to pack.
The young man
Picks up his fiddle
And places it
Back into
The imitation
Alligator case.
The island
Now is sinking
Beneath the blue sea. And
The life plot thickens.
Wait.
We have forgotten
Our footsteps.

We must cover them up
To
The post office.

EXERCISE: Create the beginning, middle, and end of a relationship in a poem.

Opening the mind to poems means listening to dialogue. Quite early in my life I found out that people can speak in poems. I try to get patter in poems. And open my mind to other people speaking. An odd example of this is in my book *The Vaudeville Marriage*:

Las Vegas

My nightclub comedian
Can no longer be found
In the Garden of Eden
Making a call
Across the country to his girl,
Can no longer be seen
In the sauna baths
Where he sat,
A great man
Sweating out his dreams.
He has left his golf course
And deserted his voice teacher,
He's forgotten his elocution lessons
And singing teacher.

His lips
Turn upside down,
His pompadour is gray.
All of his combs
Fall down.
My conceited Happy-go-lucky
Can no longer be found in the Eden Garden
Where he was the great tree and the snake,
And joker, make no mistake, he was Adam and Eve too.

He's on the telephone——Hello? Las Vegas?
Upside-down world,
Glittery old horseshow world,
Open-door fun palace
Promising stargazing and learning machines,
Gag world open twenty-four hours a day
For mad conversations,
Dream center, mad booth of lemon kings
And roulette-mongers,
Place of winnings and losses,
Wonderland of cactus and roses,
Golden Nugget Singing Eden.
I hear him
Braying in his flat voice:
    I gotta go now.

In My Sleep

The child tells his story.
The ladybug is his friend.
The spirit is his enemy.
The caterpillar eats the moth.
The careers of Barnum and Bailey and the Ringlings
Are depressing the children's government.
The top! The top! He knew it
Would spin forever. Animal acts: He
Could tame a flea. Whip
The clown. Frighten the lion
Out of his crib. The life of a cowboy——
Who is that in the saddle?

Winter

The laughter of the comedian
Is a turning point
And the last thing in my mind.
I can't stand
Up to the patter
Of the lonely comedian.

In Manhattan
Snow was forecast by
The radio. But never
Appeared.

The snow will see me out. But
After that——?

More than the snow is falling.
The world's doing pratfalls
And for all I know
Blessings
And bruises are all mixed

Up. I'm breaking up
With the stand-up comedian——
A comedy I seem to confuse
With the end of the world.

"I'm not falling apart,"
I say into the telephone
To the voices that talk back to me,

"But tumbling into a sea
Where I keep my head just
Above water."

EXERCISE: Write a poem in which conversation appears. Have a voice other than the voice of the narrator in the poem.

Centering for me means stripping the mind of nonessentials. And connecting images without apparent reason. The connections of the unconscious can tell us more about the secrets of poetry than we can begin to "think" out. Here is an early poem about growth, but growth is expressed by "the flame":

In the Flame

Bad blood, I have my right hand in the sun. I burn
My hair, my arms, my back, my face, my name,
O I have my God-hand at last in the fiery flame.
I enter light! (I have put on
The tennis sneakers of swift martyrdom.)
I run past palaces and pensions,
Past lost hotels, public Italian johns,
Past the limp bodies of the Acheron.
For I had wanted always to attract,
Not the quick pinches of the maniacs,
The selfish hands of flesh-mongers and quacks,
The selfish ones (Always the ego cracks!)
I would go whoring with the zodiac—
And I shall ride beyond
Deodorants, the clean pillows and quilts,
The shared bath towel, the box of cleaning salts
(For this is not the heart of love that feasts
On someone's marriage sheets)
Though flesh has held me with its feather fingers, I am gone.
Now I have my right hand in the sun.

EXERCISE: Open the mind to an intense experience and try to metamorphize the experience so that the "pain" and "revelation" can be described by another like experience. Tell about one thing by telling about another. Just as the *flame* becomes all of life's experience create a poem where you create your own version of fire.

Opening the mind often means becoming aware of the senses—becoming aware of feelings and of temperatures. Hot and cold—the winter and fall—all help to create a scene. In a poem about the death of my Aunt Moll I begin a poem with winter.

My Baby Aunt

In the cold air
Of this terrible Winter
I say good-by to my Baby
Aunt, youngest of five
Sisters and brothers, now
Made up in her casket,
Waiting her turn to be buried
When the gravedigger strike
Is settled. But I have been
Saying good-bye to her
For years—her lovely diction
Slurred in the telephone—
Telling me "How good
Everyone was to me at
Bellevue" and repeating

Alone   Alone
To final switchboards
Of the last
Hotels.

I trace the map: here is
A life, here is some scenery
In the country, the city, a
Cascade of furriers, meals, concerts,
Bars, and the great big
Artificial pearls. Here is a visit from
Me with a present, here is a celebration
For her newborn child, two children,

A husband. The country of my childhood
Where I go shadowing my glamorous
Baby Aunt.

"Not every life is a catastrophe, but most
Lives are," I think, uncomfortable on my
Bridge chair, locked in a modest room
Of the West Side's Riverside Chapel. There
Is no window at my Aunt Moll's funeral.

I listen to the iced voice
Of the old stranger
Performing his liturgy for the dead. I
Read the Bible to myself, instead, poems
In my mind, shutting out his sound.

My young Aunt Moll sat looking in the
Mirror of the medicine cabinet, curling
Her eyelashes and allowing me—an eight-
Year-old brat—
To use the eyelash machine and curl
My own. I see Aunt Moll performing the
Ritual of the mask—first pancake makeup
With a sponge—then orange lipstick-rouge
And powder. I was eight. I knew
Something was the matter! I stood on my toes
And tried on jewelry—great purple glass
Rings rimmed by diamond chips. I rubbed
Her Pongee lipstick on my lips.

I forget—try to forget—
My "accidents" when I was too frightened
To sleep alone and she took me into
Her bedroom to sleep in her double bed. Wetting
Her sheets, waiting for her to come home,

I covered the sheets with her towels. Suddenly,
She opens the bedroom door, turns on the light,
Forgives me, tells me about her date,
Turns off all the lights. She's had too much
To drink. Sweet liquor's
On her breath
Inside the wet bed we hug and fall into sleep.

EXERCISE: Use one of the seasons as a way of setting a mood for a poem. Let the season gradually become a part of the poem.

Open the mind to details. Specific details. And odd descriptions. In the following poem I talk about an old man but end by describing a rare bird. The poem is really about Henry Miller, the writer, but ends by being about the lemur from Madagascar.

This Summer I Am Naked in California

Taking off your clothes
In California
Is not like getting undressed
In another place. The ripe
Sun says, "No,
You cannot just admire
Me. You must live with
Me. Take me into your
Body. Sleep close to me."
Here there are no
Buttons and buttonholes.
Everything slides down
From the shoulders.
There's no family. No
Memory. And if money

Talks it does not
Talk to me. Here there

Is strength. Anatomy,
The worship of
Green vines of the body,
The stomach churns
Sunflowers, weeds,
And the eyes are clean.

Explain it?
The mild determination
That we have to be
Alone——
To discover our ears
And creases of the arm
As if we were examining
Terrible, strange,
Sting-proof maps of the skin.

If I am ever lost
Look for me in that land
Where the new body begins.
Where the evening
Lasts until midnight
And the mind is flesh.

Look for me
In that place
Of the Palisades
Where the Glass Chapel
Mirrors the moon.

Where the sea-houses
Have creaking doors
That are always open
And the sand is there
With thousands and thousands
Of beds.

Where we stare for hours
At the sun, frightened by no one.
Where the light
Breaks open our palms
And our lifelines
Run down to the sea.

Where the ankles
Are soft as birds' nests.
Where the frozen flowers
Bloom.

Where we run out of tears—
Dreaming always of making love.
Making love with the right side
Of the moon. Where we
Run out of signs and sleep
In the deaf ears of skin.

Now, can you tell me
Why there is reason
To weep?

Even the vulture
Is bent on becoming
More than just carnivorous:
His red neck
Is paved from the brilliance
Of the sun.

At night
There's the sound
Of the shell
Beating as strong
As the heart.

Nothing is human.
I become a ripe plum.
I become mango
And seed.
I burst into who I am.

In California
An old man stands, naked,
In front of his mirror
Saying, "I have
Given the poor
Everything and
Now I am truly rich."
He reminds me
Of the lemur
From Madagascar
Who has prospered,
Unmolested,
In his isolated domain. Yes. We are out here drowning——
Arms embrace
The sunlight.

EXERCISE: Write about a person and go from the general description to a very specific one in which you compare this person to an animal, vegetable, or mineral.

Open the mind to landscape. Think of yourself as a painter of people.

Arriving in Guadeloupe

I find
A small town called Gosier where
The people live this way: There are winding
Streets that go up and down hill, tin
Roofs in the sun, and schools
Separated from the street by screens.

Behind the screens children
Are singing about animals. They carry
Notebooks, lined and empty, in their arms.
They wear yellow woven hats,
Starched shirts and dresses. Crayons
Are sold in the General Store. So are rubber
Bands and water colors and other important
Things I cannot live without: feathers,
Mirrors, ribbons.

In Guadeloupe I have excellent dreams.
I redesign the buildings of my life. I meet
Again the people I have loved deeply. The
Days in boarding school appear to me
Better than they used to be: I am on the
Hockey team, I hear every record clearly
As I dance during social hour, I relive
Each day of my life, each day as right
As a leaf. I am sensible, passionate,
And I know what to do with my time. But cannot
Stay.

EXERCISE: Pick a small town that you have visited and describe it the way a painter might describe the town. Open the eyes to really *see* what the people look like.

When one is writing, everything can become one's teacher. Jerry Rubin writes in *Growing Up at Thirty-Seven*, "Pain had become my teacher." But one learns through pain, hunger, frustration, joy, aging, birthing, rejection, celebration—how to sharpen one's understanding and self-wisdom. There are people who close themselves from these experiences—they cannot face their feelings. Those who have the courage to face them can write. Writing is really, for me, the art of courage. To learn how to write is the same as saying, "How do I open myself up?"

Some of the myths about writing have kept people from writing. The myth of the writer as "traveler"—the debauched false myth of the writer created by a few examples of the writer as tragic heroine or tragic hero. The real voyage is into the self. Emily Dickinson lived in a small room but experienced everything. But Emily Dickinson read many books. Which brings me to another exercise. The most important exercise—reading.

To learn how to read, to learn from what others have written, is very valuable. To be inspired by the best poets, to read critically and to study the writing of others, is to have silent teachers who are always available.

When I was beginning to write seriously—that is to say, regularly—I gave myself the exercise of answering some of Shakespeare's sonnets. In that way I taught myself to rhyme. Imitation is the beginning of finding one's own voice. Each book can be a swami. Each book a teacher. In the end, we teach ourselves. Each poem and song teaches us how to write another poem and song.

CHAPTER TWO

Two Words

WHEN YOU WRITE, ALL YOU use are words. Words used for themselves, as in the incantations of primitive people, can have their own rhythms. Nursery rhymes and nonsense words can, in streams of thought, convey their own world. There's a sense in nonsense. Words without apparent meaning can have their own meaning. Thus uses of puns, rhymes, calls, sounds, can come from a mystical part of the brain—buried thoughts come pouring out through streams of consciousness in the same pattern as dreams. Language seen as a dream with sound can be a way of knowledge—removing thought to gain a closer access to thought.

Originality is an escape from repetition. Words are the key to originality. How to find words? As a poet I have been a hunter of words—I have investigated vocabularies. All vocabularies are the source from which language is gathered. The vocabularies of the street, the kitchen, the cinema, the nursery school, the technology of satellites, of horses, plants, psychoanalysis, Marxism, anthropology, mathematics—all words are tools for originality.

Words can be used as propaganda. Commercials have become the new poetry—pushing products on TV the new aesthetic. "To be or not to be" has become "Good to the last drop." Commercials in our society have replaced poetry. Instead of original feelings, we have proscribed feelings.

You wonder where the yellow went
When you brush your teeth with Pepsodent.

Rhythm is now a tool used for memory. If you can rhyme it, you can remember it. Slogans:

Promise her anything but give her Arpège.
If I have only one life to live let me live it as a blonde.
Put More Joy in Your Life.
Come to Marlboro Country.

These are the poems—the corporate poems spelled out in our homes, on our highways. Corporations realize the power of words. Advertising agencies become the seers and poets. We are nourished by the wrong poems, the wrong words. Our Globe Theater is now the Networks. A poem should stimulate some sense of living and being alive. Words should be reclaimed from the advertising agencies, the corporate seers, who bill their clients in the millions for the poems which they create that stimulate nothing but want.

The function of the poem and the poet is to reclaim language from the media that use words not as a means of communication, but as a means of selling. We live in a world of special words. What is law school but a learning of legal vocabularies? What is a doctor? A person with a medical vocabulary who understands the function behind all those words. The world of computerized technology has its words—or languages—which change constantly. Fortran (a computer vocabulary) turns into Cobal (another computer technology). It is almost as if the very specialness of our society has trained people to *keep out* of specialties by making the language arcane, secretive, and difficult to understand.

The poet must see through all this by word collecting and creating lists of his own. In the poem "What the Old Man Left Me," I took the ordinary words that made lists out of spools of thread:

What the Old Man Left Me

There was an old man.
He died.
Only painters came to his funeral.
They sat down. Funeral voices:
"He was here yesterday. Now he is gone."
They all had a gargantuan lunch
Talking about painters, colors,
Themselves among the peacocks.
"This is the way the old man would
Want it to be"—Nothing
At all about the almost
Forgotten old man
Except that he was filled
With spirit, filled with health,
Filled with that crazy kind of joy.
He left me, as a gift,

A basket filled with thread. Hundreds
Of spools—now in hiding—
Lost in the closet—what did
I do with that gift?—I cannot sew.
Hundreds of spools, safety pins,
Needles, straight pins,
All in a gift lost in the closet.
I remember a sewing machine
Of my grandmother's—a Singer
A thousand gleaming needles
With huge eyes—one for heavy
Cloth—one for silk—
She'd put the needle in
The black machine—thread the needle
With a hundred spools of thread
And then all morning long
        tap tap tap

Putting needles through
Silk and calico, linen and rayon too.
Where is that life where
Things out of raw stuff are made?
Little blouses, underpants, hems sewn,
As if a single shawl
Were enough to make the afternoon,
As if life had its own meaning
That she knew as she kept on sewing.

I sit all morning
At this machine
Stitching up my seams. Typing
Wounds and memories
On this odd machine
That stitches up my dreams.
Out of the great ribbon mouth: Cotton

Images, velvet fantasies,
Fear and odd words spout.
I write of insects and spinnerets,
Of spiders, write of the great
Mass of the sea.

EXERCISE: Create a poem whose strength comes from a list.

Names can be words. In the poems that I write about girlhood and boarding school
I use real names to evoke the past.

Boarding School

Pee-wee, Tut-Tut, Jumbo-Jelly—all wild
Boys. Blond lion girl friends
Combing out their hair
Scratching with their hands. Are you afraid
Of that? Of what?

Childhood. Gangs
Turning math shelters
Into caves and Miss Fowles
Breaking through Math
Bushes with her whip
Of bright red pencils. Mad

Pavilions. Tennis
Brawls. Umbrella trees.
The empty tables
Of the dining rooms.
Cloak rooms and

The boys
Silent on the assembly porch.
So silent now. Why don't they

Holler and scratch?

I hid in the English
Shelter to recover and weep.
The books were growing
Sticky at the roots. And I hide from
Them. Pee-wee brats

Who tag me in dreams, back and forth, back and forth.

EXERCISE: Take real names of people you know and incorporate these names into
the poem.

Using odd words—almost in a surrealistic way—can be helpful also. Odd pieces of
conversations, nonsense words, are blown up and enlarged.

Riverside Drive

Crossing the Drive
The nurse told her future: "When you grow up
You'll be a baboon."

Her parents pretended they were not happy
Piled up like rowboats lying on their sides
And picked themselves up for new boats and correspondents.

And she saw
Many boarding schools. And dreamt of tugboats.
Later still, sun. And a kidnap:
Nothing is as important as a pencil. Write this down.

At that moment
Saved by the boy scouts who happened
To be marching in the hills during
Her kidnap. New correspondences

And college. And a battered man, a quack in a hotel

Room saying, "When I write
I never put all my eggs in one basket." Voyages. Birds
Wore tweed flat hats with tiny beaks.
She stared, that year, at jawfuls of the sun.

EXERCISE: Write a poem where odd fragments of words and conversations add to the musicality and strangeness of the poem. Create them so they do not have to fit—they do not have to have logic. Let them have a strange logic of their own.

Specific descriptions, or use of words, means getting into the soul of another person, animal, or thing. Often one can collect specific categories of vocabularies. I remember one summer that I lived in Ossining and I lived next to a gardener. This gardener taught me all new garden words, out of which I painstakingly gardened and planted poems.

Vegetables

Whatever it is that I know
Is involved in the knowledge of vegetables.

The tomato is ripe. I am ripe also.
My life tied up with vine and stalk.

It is not enough to praise them. I must know them.
I hunger the way of broccoli—its
Sensual flower.

Pods come out of the earth.
I burst out of myself. The cabbage
Opens in my own
Eye, ear, and spine. The

Harvest!
End of Summer

"Why have you come here alone?" asks the pear,
Turning around in the sun. "I'm leaving
Everyone," I said, all summer, babbling to
Dragonflies, while frogs instead of swans
Take over the pond. An Italian gardener,
Annunziato, comes on Sundays to pull weeds
Out of the earth while wrinkles grow in
Weeds around his mouth.

I have pulled out of the garden
Ripe squash, dill, and lettuce
As we bury summer in our salads. The
Great white lily casts out its purple
Tongue as if to tell me, "We are here
But we are fragile and we'll soon be gone."

EXERCISE: Pick a category such as the garden and write words suggested by the new names that you learn. Or look at the garden section of the newspaper and find words that you don't know to spark garden poems. The same can be true to write about automobiles—look in the car sales section of the paper and collect automotive words.

Words have different tones of voice.

Be sensitive not only to tones but to "attitudes" projected by words. A medical journal has a serious tone. It is the grown-up tone of the specialist.

EXERCISE: Write a professional poem. A poem like a doctor talking. Try for the tone of the expert.

The childlike tone is the one that I enjoy. William Blake had this childlike tone in so many of his poems. Often I look to myths and nursery rhymes or stories about aborigines for a point of view. Poems are often like extensions of fairy tales—where words are simple.

Confessions from the Old Woman in a Shoe

There was an old woman who lived in a shoe
What did she do? What did she do?

She brought up her children, she wondered for a month
If she was going to go on living or give it all up—

She became forever joyful when she looked up at the sun
Or put her hands on fresh flowers, picking them.

She looked at her body and felt it was a shame
That her breasts were larger than when she was very young,

She wondered what she was doing with her life
And if in the end she had done right

She tried to develop her body, head, and mind
And to take care of money and come on time

And mostly she tried to keep her body young
And write songs which would one day be sung.

And as she got older in a rage
And saw blood upon the page
She loved more furiously than the wind
And loved more than the stories ever said.

EXERCISE: Pick a nursery rhyme and begin a poem that way.

Now try to think of a myth that you like which will spark a poem.

The Keys

Remember the immaculate King of Thule
Who ran away from his city every night

To embroider a sail in his tower? The winding spool
And the thread were his only delight
As he sang a song to himself of love and the sun.
I have trailed love down
To the end,
And under the sun
I have heard what the ear refused,
What the eye could not see,
What the mind takes down at night like embroidery.
In a sense, I have been by myself
And have sewn up my grief.
And then?
("Descend," says the King)
To the coral reef.

Electra

Electra, do not weep. If you had seen
A mule upon the bed sheets of the Queen
You might have been amused. The child is seer
To jests of vision, and the child can bear
Murder, hoofmarks, the awful slaying,
Queen's laughter, the lover braying;
This kingdom of the animals has been
Subject of the stubbornness of sin.
Child, why do you weep? The burro lies
Down in the dung of tragedy to please.

EXERCISE: Choose a hero of a nursery rhyme and myth and use him or her to begin a poem and as a way "into" the poem.

Mixing metaphors is often just mixing vocabularies. When I wrote "Conversations in a Department Store," I mixed the vocabulary of the kitchen and the department store.

Conversations in a Department Store

Remember the cook who was so bad
He jumped out the window?
Everything turned out wrong.
Simply, I just didn't follow the recipe
Everyone said I should.

Cooking up a scene; I began
Without quite knowing what I was doing.

Then I was crying
And people around me asked, "What's her name?"
And someone on the floor said, "Make her stop screaming."

And someone—in a new housecoat—said,
"She should lie down," and then
The police came. It was all pretty embarrassing.

When I'm at the police station
I try to control myself. No one protects you

Unless you look calm. I protest, "Sorry, Lieutenant, I
Didn't know what I was doing,

I really didn't die,
I only pretended to." It was lovely making believe I was dead—
I looked in the mirror and said, "With so much love to live for—
Really now!"

And it ends with my cooking up something about being sad.
It is only because women are hysterical
When no one waits at home to rub them down
With conjugal castor oil or say, "The meal was good, wasn't it—
Now how is everything?"

I'm sick of New York. That's why I often go shopping.
"The life of this woman hangs off the rack of infinity."

EXERCISE: Pick two different worlds (with their own vocabularies) and bring them together.

Gathering sea words can create sea poems. Once I read through many seabooks to get my words—as precious to me as experiences.

Above Sea Level

Living new lives
Above sea level, we have forgotten
Undersea landscapes.
Tidal zones fall like towers
At the ocean's rim.
The sea divides itself into three realms:
The Zone of the Shallow Seas, the Zone of Light,
And, beneath that, the end of the sea—
That secret and silent Zone of Perpetual Darkness. These
Zones are no longer our concern.
Slowly we came to this gentle place,
Walking past stones, trees,
Dry earth, shacks, layers of garbage,
And were stared at
By hill people. They dared us to take
Root in the earth, dared us to break
Like new flowers without stalks. They saw us
Ascending.

Once water was necessary. We farmed the sea,
Hauling out food
From salinity. Mud, fish
Gave us our lonely lives. Waves and the tides—
Starfish, scallops,

Crabs, mussels, sea pork,
Rockweeds, and shells sharp as razors—
Gave us our living.
Now we no longer dream of sea palms,
Our memories have burned out sharks,
The feeding frenzy of killers.
We have ascended through sea weather
To the top of this mountain. Here grass
Blows in green waves,
Light falls on our mouths like rain, and
Nets of white clouds tighten around our lives. We
Are free of the extremity of the sea! Free
To live with our calm self-nature. Now—
Farewell to bleeding whales,
Oil-bearing targets for whalers' harpoons.
Our net is tightened. If we leave now,
It is not for the sea—but for the endless path
That will raise us even higher
Above sea level.

EXERCISE: Find a book on the sea and write down as many sea words as can be found. Create a poem around these words.

W ords can be motifs of change. Metamorphosis is the essence of nature, and with change words change.

The Spy

At home for a week I have been spying on fruit.
In the immense bowl the fruit has ripened
And begins to change. The colors darken at
Their edges and turn black. New shapes
Explode and warp—adding new odors
To our rooms. Sap falls out of their skins,
And, at a certain point, they change

Their shape entirely, becoming both
Substance and sap. They are so
Magically changed
When they have been in a room too long. I watch
These shapes changing from green to a darker
Green—yellow into black, orange into
Black, as if all bright colors must go, finally,
Into darkness, burst, or turn to seed.
I wonder if
All trees
Are offering only a pure excuse for words—as if
Language itself were falling
From the trees, apples
No more than the boundaries of words. Ripeness.
                                        Language.
Metamorphosis. This is what I am spying on, sitting
Patiently with silent flies,
Watching these forms of life turn mad and giddy.
Mangoes, custard apples turn, unbend,
And all become something else.
If only there were a perfect word
I could give to you—a word like some artichoke
That could sit on the table, dry, and become itself.

EXERCISE: Write a poem of growth—describe a caterpillar that becomes a butterfly. Notice that with the metamorphosis of the object or insect written about, the language becomes different also. The eye and the ear combine.

Often poetry has been stilted because it does not use the vernacular of everyday words. In "Songs in Easthampton" there are many levels on which the poem can exist. On the first level, the poem is about memory. On another level, it is a poem in which the very everydayness of things intrudes on the subconscious—where reality makes its own statement in everyday words.

Songs in Easthampton

Memory kills for a moment.
There still remains
The never-resting mind
So that one can't escape
And the past comes round again.

I see a small house in the fields
And neighbors walking by
And a young girl calling to her love
Across the world to find him
And eyes that cried, and throats that laughed
And poems sung, and birdcall and plans.
It was all so long ago
Before my new life came
And days went by so quickly then
And I never learned
I didn't know I lived
In imperfect paradise.
Forget this game. Get dressed
You're late for dinner.
It's all long ago.
But the past comes back
The echo of some fat Mecox duck
As a call comes from its neck.

Comb hair.
Put on shoes.
Look in mirror.
Kill memory.

EXERCISE: Take phrases from everyday life, unselfconscious uses of irrelevancies, banalities. Turn those phrases into parts of the poem.

Another way of using words is to borrow from the past. In "A Song to Myself to Keep Singing," the language of the ancient bards is played upon. Here the words are purposely out of date—to oppose contemporary moments with another kind of English—a jumble of American English and old English. This adds to the multiplication effect of time past and time present. A conflict of styles can have its effect.

A Song to Myself to Keep Singing

Are you loveless or lovelorn?
Yours be love tomorrow morn.

The true story of fantasy will take place
The world will be so high——
Your eyes will never fill with tears
Never again cry.

Tomorrow to the loveless
The love will come tomorrow.

So let the loveless promise not to die——
Hold on to each day dearly
For love, great love is coming surely.
Tall swans will dance in numbers,
The owls and doves will mate
And all that once was promised
Will come to pass——

Hug and laugh and do not despair
Sing in the gutters and love comes, I swear.

Odd words are valuable in poetry. One, "agog" used in the next poem, fuses emotionally the meaning of the poem.

X Ray of the Woman Artist at Forty

I lob into the sun
And read my notebooks
Writing memory down
For no-one's eyes but mine.
The sun hides in the sky
And somewhere in my mind
All of my life goes by
In an odd yellow design.

Once upon a life agog
When I was young and every thigh a lesson
I stepped into the nude and dwarfed in poison

Once upon a life agog
I found lust flowing in my loves and pair
And truth: I would not want that life again.

My eye is sharpened now, after the rain
I see the bearded Iris shine in glory
And love's patience is mine. Love my life story.

I live for rainy days for love and jog
Into my days but once a life agog
I sat and waited for adventure, bliss,
Age crept upon me with the rays of sun
And like beauties life was undone.

As silly women wait for love and fame
Time does its dance leaving its prints upon
The thigh, the eye, the lips, the legs, the arm
And I say "I'm content to let life pass"
And weep myself alive and love to laugh
I lob into the sun

And write my books
As love goes through my vines of flesh, life
Atrophies, life burns, life passes by

But once agog a life age
There was no stronger eye.

EXERCISE: Write a poem about the vibrancy of life using nonsense invented words juxtaposed with a line of thought.

William Carlos Williams wrote, "Certainly a large part of my pleasure in reading poetry comes from an escape from trite forms."

Autobiography

I begin with a miracle.
Though an intellectual one.
I begin with reading books all day
And reading my own dreams.
I begin with waking up
And fashioning new words
And opening my mind
To nonsense all day long.
I begin with listening
To things my grandmother said
And wondering why
Conversations were stupid,
I begin with feeling too much
With a heart like a huge pouch
I begin with staying awake too much
And hanging around the house——
When life was fine for other girls
My life was lived in myth
And all my days exposed
On the shaggy hills of heart. Bare rock

Under my hands—plants singing in the air
And all as if it was
Meant for my own ears.

I live unsheltered now
In the hills of the heart
And words stick like amoebas
Right into my skin

And underneath my skin
My death is open to me
And I can't forget my birth
Or the ache of all the others.

EXERCISE: Do away with the trite autobiographical poem as it is known and invent new thoughts about yourself. Write your autobiography in a short poem, alternating rhythms, rhyme and nonrhyme.

Louis Zukofsky has stated that his desire was to "record and elate for all time poems based on nothing less than the world, the entire humanly known world."

EXERCISE: Write a cosmic poem. Read Nigel Calder's *Violent Universe* and borrow astronomy terms from this book and write poems about sun, stars, galaxies, and the universe. Write poems about the explosion of the universe. Then about the explosion of simpler feelings. Let explosive words into the poem. Borrow worlds. And astronomy terms such as visible light, ultraviolet light, x rays and gamma rays, quasars and helium. Be an astronomer of words.

Just as the galaxy is held together by gravity, poems are held together by the energy of words. Just as there are thousands of millions of galaxies, there are thousands and millions of words in combinations which create poems. The energy of the common slang has a potency of language that is amazing. Don't be "afraid" of slang.

Cry from the Hamptons

Yes I'm
In the world
Of old farts
And young kunts
And great painters
With cigars
And a couple of drunks
And widows
And the married
And the young and the striving
And the whole world
Under the sea
And a dram world
And a dream world
Tennis courts float through
The grass
And lunches tinkle on the meadow
Conversation
Stops
When love is mentioned
And Paradise
Casts its ancient shadow.
Were those peacocks
The old man had in a cage?
Was that sperm
The girl swallowed?
Was that fear?
Was that age?
I'm in the Shorelap,
The Wingscape, the Nightbloom—
I see it happen
Before my eyes
And I sing in the rain all alone.

EXERCISE: Mix vulgarities with soothing rhythmical words.

I try not to write and only write when I have to. For the past year I have written no poems at all, knowing that the necessity of writing would come upon me, that I would need, one day, to be delivered of words. Or that words would "come through me" as if I were a vessel through which they, like water, had to pass. That is why one teaches oneself "techniques" of poems. All the techniques—the writing in forms, the breaking of forms—exist so that when the words are in your head you have the technique to write them. What happened to me in East Hampton was that I had been thinking about love and age. I observed many couples who were paying a large price for the coupling. I experienced an odd freedom in not being part of a "couple" or being part of anything. The words rattled around in my head. I allowed myself to be "delivered" of the following poem:

Looking in the Mirror

How weird to sit in front of a mirror
Seeing myself not as the "other"
But as someone who has aged, whose face
Once childlike now seems older
And to know, with sadness, I have gone
From girlhood to the middle years. Beyond
All this the sea of the wild Hamptons
Beats its restless waves against the curls
Of clam white shells and sexual young girls.

Never have I felt the rage
To live more violently inside my arms
Or felt the muscles in the legs
Ache more to run, ache more to go beyond
The simple boundaries of life as it is.

Beyond me stretch a million love affairs
With those who may be kind and may be jealous
Unknown relationships that may stretch me

Marrow, bone and heart. The future sees my child,
My one love, growing into boyhood and my work
Mean more to me than ever—words I work with
Precious as any lover.

At forty I can whisper to my wealth
Of secrets—I have known all that life can
Offer—poet, lover, mother, I have tasted
Everything—run everywhere—strange cities,
Odd seas, strangers I have slept with—
And with it all—the tragedy and
The heart knotted around itself—
I have kept that one precious thing—not love—
Not sensuality—but being free.

This poem led to others. It was the "seminal" poem—the words that started freeing me of everything I felt.

George Sefaris says, "While translating one learns one's own language."

I often do an odd kind of word research. I force myself to write poems from the phone book. The classified yellow phone book excites me. My heart starts to pound ridiculously. So many words locked up in that book! My first example of doing this is in this very early poem of mine, "To the Fire Dancers."

To the Fire Dancers

I spoke to the Marriage Dancers, whispered to them
To crawl out of the crumbling hotels
While the earthquake shook
The island of Manhattan with a gong
That might have been
The Bell Telephone ring.

What was I saying to the Marriage

Dancers? I was saying, "Get out quick"—that is to say,
Get the hell out of this island that is itself
A sort of hell. Get out of the telephone directory,
For God's sake,
Get out of the Manhattan Yellow Pages—out of maps,
Get out of Convent, Lexington, Pleasant,
Get out of Boiler Repairing, Washington Machine and Welding Works,
And Tom Wizard's Auto Repairs,
Get out of Chemicals, out of the Kramer X-Ray Co.,
Jump out of Heat,
Jump from Precision Heat to Insect Killing Devices,
Get out of Lightning and Limousines and Wheel Chair Travelers
And the Pioneer Business Record Center,
Marriage Dancers jump from Complete Packaging Service into
The Wolfahrt Studios Incorporated, my God,
Get out of the Seafare Restaurant.

Dance out of Installations, out of the Card Dialers,
Princess Phone Wall Telephone Home Speakerphone
    Telephone
In color—can you hear me? And

The Marriage Dancers leapt out of the Yellow Pages
That were yellow flames, walking fingers, then
    walking feet, then
Dancing feet-arabesque—over the flames of
The city.

I had one more call to make and that
Was to the people on my island
Who were unhappily married
And would remain so
During the earthquake. I had to tell them
And rang them up secretly
And asked them why they moved out of each other's beds

And into each other's beds
Without hearing each other walk,
Without hearing each other speak, either
To themselves or to the other. It was
As if they were all standing
On separate balconies.

I wanted to tell these couples to stop leaving each
Other before they reached each other——
To stop pulling each other's eyelashes while tears came down. Stop
Ripping each other's tonsils when lips met,
Stop pulling at each other's sexes. The radio played
And the television and the Victrola now
Hi-fi played from several speakers. But there were no speakers.
They never spoke to each other and
That was the trouble I wanted to tell them
Before the flames began——before the earth
Opened up——they should speak and dance
With each other since they might still be dancing
Beneath the earth in sickness never in health.

But I misplaced my own voice
Somewhere in my house.
I have looked under the telephone,
Beneath two pink sofas, both stiff as lips,
Inside hatboxes, underneath my chair. And
I have searched beneath the table
And beside the lamp,
Looked through one linen closet and
The medicine cabinet,
Looked in dictionaries and in the sink
Wondering where my voice
Is hidden——to warn
The Dancers.

EXERCISE: Take the classified section of the phone book and pick out words to write with. Incorporate many of the "service" words into the poem.

Sometimes poems come out of key words. I heard the word "patience" in my mind and didn't know what it meant. The poem explained it to me:

Away Alone At Last A Loved A Long

The road goes round and round
To meet where life begins
And I'm out in the pastures
Again with foes and friends.

The lady with a mansion
Dreams of finding lovers

The painter without passion
Looks for nubile mother

The silly blonde son of a bitch
Tries to look social and rich

And the writer who sees truly
Drinks and gets unruly

But it's all in the pastures
With life going tick tock
All in the Hamptons
Where flesh has a time clock——

I see my friends grow old
Brown settles on their teeth
And the brazen girls once bold
Have grown enormous needs

Scheherazade has given up her tabs
And her thousand and one nights
Are spent in witless veils
For she's grown another chin
And doesn't look so thin
Yes, it was once my job
To dance with Scheherazade——

There's a glitter that gladdens the girl
In a life without dazzle and curl
And time lifts its sunny veils soon
For the dazzling old woman buffoon

In summer's oddball world
I wouldn't change it all for a thing
All vanity must end
And patience, patience is the main thing

T. S. Eliot, when talking about receiving manuscripts from young poets at Faber & Faber, said, "Sometimes when young people send in manuscripts they ask me, 'Am I a poet? Should I go on?' I answer, 'You're the only one to know that, you have to decide by yourself.'"

Places can create poems. So can rhyme. Rhyming words is a kind of game that often helps poems take on a magical "curing" quality. It is almost as if magical words can cure us of our own ills and insanity.

A Song for a Daffy Heart

Shall it ever be? The blood of
Paradise?

A daffy song
Sing Hey the wide merry
That life is long
And loving is crazy

A daffy song
That age always finds us
A happy song
If love cannot bind us

A simple song
To look for a lover
A zany song
If he's not uncovered

Sing songs of blood
And misunderstanding
Songs of life
And lists and of planning

Of strangers met
Who take off on airplanes
And loves we touch
And lose in the life game

A daffy song
Out in the wild Hamptons
Where life goes wrong
And still good things happen

Of strangers met
And eyes that are weeping
And days go by
Into the sun, into the blood, into

The past
Where
All songs stay at last
For keeping.

Shall it always be? The life
That's gone at last.

EXERCISE: Pick words that rhyme and write a poem using them. Alternate the rhymes with nonrhymes as in "A Song for a Daffy Heart."

Words create dreams on paper. The strangeness of a dream is often close to artifice. A dream mixes memories and obtains an event unrelated to anything that it mixes.

Song with Claws
They lived and loved and laughed and left——

And the sea went on, the green meadows bloomed
The music was written, the guests were fed
And showed around, the drink went down the throat and
The old man got sick, and the girl who got dressed got weary
And the cooks got mean and the married got bored for
The twentieth year and the young bitter man
Drank his life down and the young man dreamt in the
Heated swimming pool and the widow gave a party
And the good man, the one good man smoked a cigar while
His good wife looked at grass from a car, and the painter
Went down between the secret grasses of the sweating sea——
The old fisherman painter with the nets off his eyes
And the young woman (which used to be me)
Looked in the mirror at the person she used to be and laughed
And the little girls wore wet suits and old men
Huffed and puffed about the sea-like gulls
And the nouveau riche nagged each other about sports and got old
And the summer sun went up and down
And the tourists came——and life went on as usual through
The closed shades, and dishes were washed, eggs scrambled,
The zombies walked the beach and the beds were made
And they lived and loved and laughed and left

And the summer went on in the sea-like place where things bloomed
And I wrote my songs, nestled in the wind, and I threw my songs
Away, giving them to the salt, and I dragged my songs to shore
The way the fishermen trap the lobsters
And I saw those big red lobster songs and
Loved them.

EXERCISE: Create an entire landscape in words that evoke the time and place.

Talking about words, Jean Cocteau said, "Without puns, without riddles, there is no serious art. That is, there is only serious art. . . . Every masterpiece is made of hidden confessions, calculations, lofty puns, strange riddles."

EXERCISE: Create a poem with puns, odd landscapes, and riddles.

Exactitude of language is for me the odd commandment of poetry. I try as often as possible to find the "exact" word. This search borders on mania. I am reminded of Jean Cocteau's advice to the poet: "If someone asks me, 'What did you eat?' and I make a mistake in my answer, I will rectify it the next day even if I am taken for mad, for I believe that exactitude, even in trifles, is the basis of all greatness."

About the necessity of poetry Cocteau wrote "Poetry can seem to be the height of luxury. But its unknown necessity is revealed by the fact that it haunts the hardest souls, those least apt to let themselves be haunted."

I write often to free myself of something. To be delivered of a music that I hear in my ear. To get rid of the words that are rattling around in my head and haunting me. Recently I wrote twenty poems in one afternoon in East Hampton. I had tried "not to write them," but I kept hearing the words in my head and had no choice.

CHAPTER THREE

Subjects for Poems

WALT WHITMAN WROTE "SONG OF MYSELF"—but in a sense all of our songs are songs of who we are. Many of my own songs begin with childhood. Freud has instructed us that "it all begins with the child," but for some people the escape into childhood is a second life, a second chance to re-create what went well or what went wrong. Here is my own childhood splayed in front of me in three poems written over the years. The first poem, "Freedom," was written when I was twenty. It was about wanting to break away from childhood. The second poem, "Visions Avenue C," was written when I was twenty-five and was another vision of childhood. The final poem, "A Secret Song in the Hamptons," was written just recently—at age forty. All different versions of me using myself as subject for my own poems and visions:

Freedom

I have grown tired of the water tap,
The bowing maids, the telephone messages, the crap.
From now on I will praise the water
That flows down me and to me and from me
Marl, turf, red sod and barbed root, the dust
Are mint and sacrament.
Here is the household of the apple grass
Above the shut eye-caverns of the worm
And I know both these kingdoms of the earth.
I also know the moon. One snowy-owl
Jogs down from Canada, wing over frozen cloud.
One snowy-wolf confronts me with his open jaw
As I devour seed
Of dandelion from Queen Anne's table weed.
Surely the Khan of Tartary once dwelt
Beneath a tent of felt. O tent of felt!

Visions Avenue C

Where Puerto Ricans
Squash seeds with ripe feet

And baby Hebrews dance to school,
Their curls
Dangling from manly suede hats,
I heard a voice
Singing clearly to me: "Don't
Speak with men but with angels."

I dreamt of my dead grandfather
Who once lived on St. Mark's Place.
For a nickel he would minstrel
In the parks, or jostle hot dogs
On a wooden cart, not dreaming
That his sons could make a million.

My other grandfather plumbed most of Brooklyn.
He gave up plumbing for Show
Business. All the Broadway flops
Were hauled off in his trucks—

How can I bear to dig this warehouse up?
From now on
As I dog-step through
My city, I'll
     speak
Not to men but angels.

A Secret Song in the Hamptons

As a child I used to wonder what would I be like
When I grew up—what would I be? What would I do?
Sitting for hours in the lush of summer
Propped on a lawn reading a book—always the loner—
Away from the grown-ups or my odd girl friends
Who never cried as much or asked as many questions. In the end

I have turned out to be
This crazy woman sitting by the sea.

As a child I used to wonder what would I be like
And now, oddly, I wonder——what was I really like——
As a child——was I always afraid——
Of the things I said, of the weird impression I made——
Why did I always admire others——but sit aside——

While daring to dream of a woman that was miraculous and
Decide that would be me. I wanted to be——
To be out of boarding school, out of my country,
In love with some magical person who would hallucinate
With me.

I discovered each man to be as frail as I was——
Twirling my body around stars and beggars, poets,
Odd musicians, fiddlers, comics and rich lord of
The sea, every kind of human man——doctor, lawyer,
Movie star, self-destroyer——tasting all their dreams
Inside my mouth, their tongues inside of mine
And always running away after a time——
Looking for another——my soul-friend——my truest lover.

Now this poem should end
The way the fairy tales do——the way
Erica Jong ends her latest confession——the way
We expect things to end if we read about happy people
In *Newsweek*. Unfortunately——I have come to the conclusion
That daffy people in the mad institutions
Are happier than couples——that most people who hug each other
Are falling off cliffs. And so this Song ends with me being
Alone and overweight, getting a suntan, but having friends
Like Susan and Donald——grateful that at least
I have survived.

EXERCISE: Write a poem about your vision of yourself as a child. Another poem about growing up. Another poem about looking back.

I often write poems about what I cannot bear. A recent poem is about separation from my child:

A Song of Desperation

I knew a poet in Spain who brought up his son
And when his son went away he went on a drunk
And had a faraway look of lost oceans in his eyes
And could not focus. I felt always sorry for him and
Sensed his despair. And now——

I am that poet. Out at the Hamptons with
My child in Asia——living in Bangkok but I cannot
Hear her voice——the phones never work——and I miss
Her breath, her smell, her warm voice. Nothing
Will stop my imagination from thinking of
Her going to sleep without me near her. This is the price
I pay for a terrible freedom. Is it worth it?
Every summer I tremble myself to sleep
And miss my child so far from my love and touch.

I am desperate without the one life that matters——
I am living, but not living at the same time. Moments
Seem to stretch out into infinity and
My life will not nearly be mine until she returns. And
Still I must live, talk, eat, carry on each day

With the love of my life so many sunsets away.

EXERCISE: What pains you most? Write about that.

But my joy is often taking the muse and subject of one poem and writing a completely different poem on the same subject. As Ariel is a subject for despair, she is often the subject for complete joy:

Song of Ariel

Ariel, beloved little flesh
Over the sea in another dreaming
While I'm awake you are sleeping
Ariel of the elephant
Ariel of the buddha
Ariel of the letter and the mystical number
Sweet paddycake of flesh
And mother of me
My child, my love, all that love can be.

My own child, Ariel, has inspired many poems. Here is one of my early Ariel poems:

Thoughts About My Daughter Before Sleep

Ariel, one true
Miracle of my life, my golden
Sparrow, burning in your crib
As the rain falls over the meadow
And the squirrel corn,
While the fragrant hyacinth
Sleeps in its bed in the rich
Mud of the North, while foamflowers
Climb through small arches of rain, and the sun
Brings lilies and dark blue berries
In cluster, leaf on leaf again,
I wonder how I came to give you life.

Here, where the twisted stalks
Of deer grass zigzag

66

Branches from the tree, where
Honeysuckles trumpet, "All joy
Is in the dark vessels of the skin!"
And thorn apples open their leaves,
I marvel to have made you perfect
As a small plant, you, filled
Up with sunlight and
Fragrant as ferns.

And before snow
Covers ivy and bluet
Shall I teach you this old
Summer's lesson
About seeds? About miracles
Of growth? Here are the bursting zinnias,
Asters, prongs of phlox—
Shall I wake you?
Take you out of sleep
And roll you in the apple fields?

And through you
I am born as I lie down
In the seedbox of my own beginnings,
Opening the wild part of me,
Once lost once lost
As I was breathing
In the vines of childhood.

I like to choose as subjects for poems unusual or traumatic events and then find the oddness in them, the unreality of their terror. Here is a poem about abortion:

How We Get Rid of Our Childhood

"Get rid of your childhood your childhood your swanhood."
"It's not so easy." Getting rid of a not-wanted

Wild feathered childhood. Not so easy
Varnish and soft pillows
Getting rid of that swanday those long days
Not so easy. Getting rid of a swan.

Tell us how to begin. I was not shown
A way to speak of pain
When we were young. Embryos, fighting to be born,
Say, "Time to hatch your life." But where do we begin?
I was not shown
A way
Although I listened to the lizard's tongue
And heard the stars lamenting as they glide
Into the foaming zodiac.

And when the time came
I rode to Newark in a rented car,
Reading a book. Juggling up and down,
I was still, if you can imagine, reading
Fairy tales. I read of the Princess of China

And the Princess September. I read of the Fishbone
Princesses and of the Princess Etcetera. At the

Newark Airport
Two nurses carrying
Pocketbooks picked me up. They

Blindfolded me. Beyond my blinds
I saw houses
Of white brick, plaster, orange cement. One building
Was called "The Caprice." I
Thought of the Princess of Newark. The Swan Princesses. Varnish

And soft pillows.

EXERCISE: Pick an agonizing event. Write a poem that is an *agon*.

We do not know ourselves as well as we think we do. Poems are a form of investigation into our own private lives. "The Inheritance" is a poem about change.

The Inheritance

What I wanted
Was to be myself again
On a Monday morning, to
Wake and wash with cold water
And soap, to dress
Swiftly and walk without
Thinking
Where I came from, who I was,
To be silent and
Saved
From the long days of myself.
It no longer mattered
If I burned, bursting,
Then catching fire. It
Was enough to have
Known the war within
Myself and to be tired—
To be sick of the
Boundaries—to have
Lived in the calendar of the
Brain where one meets
One's self each day in a talking
Mirror and says, "How long
Are you here for? When
Will the war be over?" I wanted
A sea change, a place
Where things grew into

Secrets of color,
A place I imagined of festivals,
Rocks, brilliant
Reptiles, trees
And serious things—wind bells
That chime—a place
Where I could be useful.
We moved, quite suddenly,
To the Colony.
I saw ancient women
In their tennis suits
Playing all afternoon. Their men
Played Business, Journalist,
General—others were
Involved in Domestic Monopoly—
And some played
Sailor on the sea. I lived
In their fashion,
Going in and out of the
Moments. If it were not
For the fish
And melons,
For the queer atonal
Music and water slipping
In the cracks of houses,
Olive fresh-water snakes,
The strangeness—
I might have
Become a part of the Colony,
Seeing myself in that life
In which all things
Are at the height of themselves.
I might have eaten mangoes,
Had my picture taken,
Written postcards to friends

Announcing my recreation, gone
On gaping at bar girls
And bargains, and having
Coats made by
Overnight tailors.
But I must tell you this:
One morning I woke up
And entered life;
I ran quite swiftly through the mountains,
Passing the palm trees and civets,
Watching harvests
And children
All in the ripeness of summer. It
Was then
I inherited joy
The way one inherits a fortune.

EXERCISE: Write a poem about a life-change.

Events can inspire poems. Here is a poem I wrote about the moon landing as if it were seen by someone in an insane asylum:

In a Cosmological Hospital

There was a young girl who sat in a sanatorium
Watching the men land on the moon. She had watched
Herself split down the middle with a crack, she
Had heard the shattering, she was being
Treated for shock. All the king's horses and all
The king's men were trying to put her together again.
She saw the rocket lifting in the sky. It was, she
Told me, "Like watching the Empire State Building
Taking off for a day." She also changed the station
And saw young men wearing bathing suits and
Carrying on their heads great gleaming surfboards

On which to ride through a wave. Then, back
Again, Armstrong was saying good-bye to the earth
And his wife. "Turn up the TV," a nervous
Woman said. The girl: "A well-known
Group of gynecologists are mending me. Sewing
Me. Asking me to please sit still." At the hospital
Real men, not men in her imagination, were
Landing on the moon. "Make it strange," said Tolstoy,
Writing about the art of fiction. What could
Be stranger? She sat with her mind fixed to the machine
"I am sick Orpheus trying to mend," one man said.
She answered, "I'm also trying to descend. I am
Beatrice watching history being born. I am
One with the lune."

EXERCISE: Take an event such as the landing of people on the moon, or a blackout, or a war—and write a poem about it. Imagine retelling the event in an odd way.

Rainer Rilke said that we would have no great poetry unless poetry serves great ends. But what are great ends?

Great ends may be the illumination of change and contradictions. For Homer great ends were the illumination of the destiny of man and how we are weak under the force of destiny. For Dante the great end was to illuminate the force of spiritual love—as perceived by Beatrice. For Rimbaud and the surrealists the great ends came from automatic writing which led to that portion of the subconsciousness which was not forced by thought—but naturally had an order of its own which the poet could bring forth by not letting thought interfere with imagination. For Wallace Stevens poetry was an illumination of the inner vision that came through speech. Poetry was also a way for the poet to cure himself. For Mao Tse-tung poetry was an inducement to action.

Modern American poetry has seen the poet disillusioned with technological society that destroys the personal life. Or, as in the case of Marianne Moore, for example, poetry is a demonstration of a fastidious and scrupulous spirit. Also, contemporary poetry has had the "self" as the subject for writing.

What is called confessional poetry or the "self as a subject" is what is interesting to me. The secrets of one's own life are often the secrets of others so that a humiliation or a fear truly expressed is almost like a case history which communicates the fears of others. Stanislavsky spoke about "particularizing" experience—giving the details. The poetry of confession and secret particularizes the poet's life.

One begins with the self as subject.

Almost all of my poems are myself observed. Puritanism has sought to eradicate the ego (a gentleman or a lady did not discuss themselves). Freud changed all this. The Kama Sutra mentality of today teaches us that the self is all we have. If one had to describe the seventies in America, one could best describe it as "Self is beautiful"—Tom Wolfe's put-down of this in the *Me Generation*. But hearing about the "me" in each of us came out of the sincere need for people to examine themselves in relationships, and in relation to the machinery and bureaucracy around them. Me does not have to be self-centered. There is nothing to be ashamed of. Everything that the "me" has felt others have felt too. I believe that if one gets in touch with the real "me" inside of us, one is getting in touch with others. The me can be childlike:

Song for Erica and Stephanie

I'll turn human actions
Into song
And poems into blood
And tell you what is good.

I'll turn the force
Into the word
And steal from the gull
And the long beaked bird.

A vision of life
That is private and long
I'll hold out to you
With my palm, with my song.

The "me" can be tormented:

Twisted Love Song
Once I lived and danced
Was joyful and happy
In that odd place of life
With clovers and poppy
The body was blood
My joy was in bed
And I ran through the fields
With a wide pregnant belly.

Once I was who I was then
And now I have changed and am who I am now
But it's all the life-song
That I sing from my gut
And from my green heart, that is twisted,
That can't get enough.

In my own work the senses become part of the poem:

I Want to Tell You
I want to tell you what it feels like not to touch.
It's terrible. Your head blows up
Until it feels like a balloon floating somewhere
And your feet are filled with helium and your light
In the sky—only nothing is there. No arm, no wrist,
No thigh. The thighs go first. Feeling gone.
Then the nipples. Then your arms.

Not to make love is unbearable.
Taking hold of the resting place you
Bob into sleep, but it isn't sleep. It isn't relief—it's
The sleep of the prisoner with the terrible bars
Of the body shining in the distance. And that's why the womb

Shines like linoleum
Under the stars, marvelous in its pursuit
Of a poor piece of flesh that will lovingly
Cover it up. Oh hear me, amazons, mistresses, wives,
Let air fly through the body, let all women dance
Into kingdoms of where living is not getting even.

EXERCISE: Write a poem about touching as if you were a blind person.

What makes a person write—beyond all this—is sensory perception plus knowledge. A poet is a specialist in everything—you cannot read enough, see enough, travel enough, feel enough, open the senses enough. To be a writer is finally to have a philosophy of life that allows you to live as fully and adventurously as you can. Nothing is wasted. Anger, frustration, sorrow, joy—all are the materials out of which a life-poem is created. Also, one must not forget that the artist is always going deep into the interior of the mind, a psychonaut discovering new places to visit. What the rocket is to interplanetary travel—that combustion of energy that gives the lift to the larger space vehicle—that's what the imagination is to the poem—a boosting of energy that carries one deep into the cosmos of the brain which is still a world to be discovered. Astronauts of the imagination—the poet goes deep into experience, penetrating into what things are—and what he or she is.

My second book of poems, *Manhattan Pastures*, was about the self recoiling from the harness of our environment. Here the "self" was not just pitted against "parents" or "home" but pitted against society. I was questioning my own ability to survive, and this questioning became the poetry.

Divorce was a theme that came into my work. Because my own parents had been divorced, and then I was divorced. I used what I knew best as a theme for the poems.

The poet matures by a willingness to take risks. You can take risks with your own life—it is really the only power that one has—over oneself—and to describe oneself. The self as an adventurer.

Celebrating Lilies

I have made love to the yellow lilies,
Turned my face against their cool skin,
Led my lips and eyes to their stamens

While I cried to see anything as bright
As these golden lilies.
How I look for them!

There are people who do not explore the in
Side of flowers, kissing them,
Resting their own tongues on their petals.
I must tell them. Where will I begin?

And I love
Earth, violently, and vegetables,
Stars, and all things that will not break.
My hair smells of melons, marl, jasmine.

The self as a sensualist tired of a world without meaning:

A History of the Opera

It was summer on Boulevard Raspail.
Our bathroom walls were peeling to light pink.
Brushes and combs were missing teeth on
The bath shelves. A box of soapflakes
Stood by the bathtub waiting to transform me.

Tacked over the sink,
Painted de Kooning wenches torn
Out of *Art News* magazine
Were staring down. They didn't like
Being placed over the sink where no one
Knew who they were.

I looked like one of them: pouting, angry, hair always messed,
Spending afternoons inside the tub
Whenever my husband took off for more than a week
On a concert tour somewhere in Lisbon or Brussels. Desperate——

I soaked in Paris. Scrubbing the loneliness
Of my skin. Frightened. I missed him
And needed the bubble baths to keep me from crying.
I sang in the daily bath. And thought sometimes of drowning.

Tub thoughts: when I was about fifteen
Some girls held a contest in boarding school to decide
The easiest way of suicide. A history major,
I quoted the Romans: "Bleeding in the bath——preferably
With slits in the arms. And loads of rose petals."
Tub thoughts: Paris——
It comes back
The bathtub filled with white detergent——Fab
Which made the bubbles in the tub as high
As an Eiffel Tower when I cried.

Now who was it
I really felt like drowning? Was it myself? My husband?
Or de Kooning?——his
Painted American women screwed up and frustrated inside his mind,
Now paper witches hanging by my tub. American
Women——locked in my bathroom——
Where they peered at my eyebrows, ears, and feet
Without the shrewdness that would make them great. O
Those young women——scrubbed and
Tubbed before they went to bed at night like children,
Washed, dressed, helped into pajamas,
Tucked into mighty dreams with creamy faces,
Saying their sexual prayers.
The painted women that I could not drown.

I became aware of needing a lover
One afternoon as I lay in the tub
And stared at my knees. As I looked at my toes
Planted near rusty fixtures,

I began thinking of a soap opera that might be called
In Defense of Love.

I then chose my lover. A modest music teacher.
I jumped out of the tub,
Rang him on the phone,
And finding him at home
Where he happened to be writing *A History of the Opera,*
I said, "All the pleasures
Of the opera are awaiting you."

He entered the bathroom elegantly,
His dyed hair smoothed by pomade, the shiny strands greased black
Over gray, his moustache
Waxed for this special occasion. To improvise: he joined me
In the tub, where I awaited him
Under the detergent.
How easy! The ecstasy—
Our electrical field of water and shock,
The short-distance field
Exposing us to
Washcloth and soap.

Somehow I want to say—to get it "across to you"—how moving
That bath was, the two of us sitting in my tub.
Those large soap bubbles in our mouths.

And ice-water changes.
Our two bodies danced in a sea of detergent
And our dangerous arias.
There were no limitations to our city
When fables and swans
Splashed in the marble.

I cloaked him in a terry-cloth robe

And lifted him, gently, from the bath.
We turned and waved good-bye

To the water.

De Kooning's maidens watched us back out of that bathroom
As we slipped from their extraordinary reach.

A self that questions marriage—the self as questioner of myths:

Adam

Dripping winters
Peer from woodwork in this fake Sistine,
Watch my muscles stretch,
My fingers rest upon the looking glass
Gripping suspect figures.
Adam in the mirror. Who am I?
I have not died, but I have seen my soul
Plunge from ceiling to the bedroom wall,
And so, when I say death, I mean each time
I've loved, and could not love, each time I've wept
And could not reach for something which leapt
Over death

Opening up the looking glass again.

A self that sees in ordinary things—an extraordinary truth. I remember going to the zoo with the poet Robert Lowell and seeing in the seals all of mankind's captivity in relationships.

Ordering one's experience is part of what one does when one is involved in poetry. The more one is in touch with oneself, the better the poem. The more one is able to draw on one's own experience, the closer one can get to an imaginative reality. I remember once asking a lover for the gifts that I had given him—back; this list became a poem—the details charged with the reality of what I felt. Details and lists can be a form of autobiography—a microcosm of a whole life lived together.

EXERCISE: Create a poem in the form of a memo to yourself.

Poetry is a way of dissecting one's own life. Remembering it and creating new meanings out of objects, feelings, places. Objects can be charged with personal meaning.

The Central Market

Women peel
Thousand-year-old eggs
By scraping off mud
From the colored shells. Under
Great fish heads bleeding
On a string, we
Are discovered walking
Hand in hand
In this market where
Everything's possible.
We have arrived
In this human place
Of sea-horse medicine
Where sugared kumquats
Shine in glass jars
And spiders and rats
Parade through vegetables. Here,
In this winding street,
A lazy boy
Holds Chinese oranges
Inside his hands
And spends all morning
With a rubber stamp stamping
Them "Sunkist" so
They'll sell for more. Here we
Touch elephant horn——black
Tusks and ivory——

Here we touch thin private scrolls
And rims of porcelain,
See wizards carve flowers
In white mah-jongg cubes. My
Senses open wide
And make me dizzy. Water bugs
That will refuse to drown
Burn on our sandals. Vendors
Show their teeth
Of golden stones. Suddenly, ducks,
Pressed with sleepy eyes,
Hang over us like rows
Of tennis racquets. Snakes
Are pulled out of
Baskets to be eaten. And the sun
Presses against us. Starting
From where we are,
Let's go down, down, down under the cabbage and
Ginger, let us escape
These ducks and taste our lives. Under
The blood of animals
Let's turn our own lives inside out,
Throwing away petals
We cannot hold—
Families, deaths, marriages—
Discarding our histories.
Those exits and entrances
We cannot explain, mistakes,
Odd people, countries
We have slept with,
Throw ourselves
Down under the dragonflies, broccoli,
Under the pythons, crushed medicines,
Spices,

While our silly tongues scratch,
Our new bodies touch,
And we are always ready to be born.

EXERCISE: Write a poem about vegetables in a marketplace.

There is everything to write about. There is nothing you can't write about. The self is projected to become everything and everyone. One exercise about taking oneself and projecting it is to go to a museum and stare at portraits. Imagine what it would be like to be that person in the painting.

I Am the White Woman of Picasso

Thick shoulders, thick fingers, large thighs,
Large breasts.
I am almost part of the white background I lounge against.
I stare at an imaginary wall.
I become the imaginary force, I am capable of illuminations.
Dreams, actions beyond belief, productions, books, children,
Tennis games—all of these acts fall from me like leaves
From a white poplar tree.
I am serenity
When you do not see me, I am jogging around the park
Breathing in gulps of fresh air as if the air itself were
Very delicious
I am part of my time.
I wrote poems. I sell dreams. I instigate children to misbehave.
I get bored easily with fools and with men who do not know
Who I am.
I am the white woman of Picasso.

EXERCISE: Project yourself inside a painting.

Another book of poems, *The Vaudeville Marriage*, was about girlhood and love disappointment. My subject matter was still the self:

Patter

Nothing is less innocent than two people
With a sense of humor. Take this young lady and
The comedian. She's intellectual. Romantic. He's almost untutored
In the finer arts: reading and writing. A realist,
He looks for his name in *Variety* and *Show Business*,
Keeps on a diet. Will not leave his wife and kiddies.
She lives alone. Suddenly gets thin. He's reading
Rimbaud. She studies vaudeville. She's making him read,
Taking him to museums. She's losing weight
And reading *Variety*. She thinks of placing
An ad in *Variety*: Young Girl Falls Flat For
Comedian. He's a looker. She's not
Show Biz. She's now wearing false lashes and
Hairpieces. Something is goofy. A show for
The Palace. He's reading
And she's writing hunks for comedians. O long
Copacabanas. How can you tell me that these people
Aren't freaks? They are not people at all.
He says he is trying to make her "more real."
She can't break through his cakewalk. She's figured
Out he was a comedian in the Garden
Of Eden. He says she has a personality that would
Revolutionize the Ice Business. She's so friendly.
He has no emotion. She has too much. He's a realist.
She's a dreamer. He wants fame and fortune. She
Wants to lead a good life. He makes her get skinny. She
Makes him lose his mind. And his zest for sleeping. Reading
All those poems. They do a man-woman act. It never
Goes over. Then they try the School Act. The Storyteller
And the Dramatic Sketch. The Stump Speech. He's
A ventriloquist. He keeps telling her what to say
And think. "Even if I wasn't married I wouldn't get married!"
Why not? "People like us shouldn't get married." Why not?

"We're not people." What are we? We are the acrobatic act
With complete somersaults.
Magicians. Wire acts . . . I tell ya
It's real hard work in Hollywood if one
Takes the profession seriously. You know all comedians
Are really tragic. I'm very strange. Silent. A freak. I don't
Belong anywhere. And have no desire to be Show Biz. I have no friends.
I'm shy. Unmaterialistic. Did you ever get those guys?
I'll go back to my life with an appreciative feeling
For having met you in person. Your act was educational
As well as entertaining. I'll look for your name and you
Look for mine. I think we should see less of each other. I'll call
Ya tomorrow. I'll really never
Make it. I'm not Show Biz.

Summer

Ho Ho for my yellow summer. But are they really funny,
The paid comedians who mock
Their desperate lives to get applause? I know
My joker is lost
Inside movie reflections of despair——
He's working in Hollywood this summer. And playing
Golf. His secret is:
He knows that he's grotesque.
Solitude's best. I spend my summer on a rented farm
Not far from a run-down golf course. Yellow's here,
Lopped in the sun. And the grass
Bending in wild hilarity
To be so green. Summer is nearly gone
Mornings I ride a yellow horse
Over the yellow field. When I arrive
At sunflowers we halt. I must slow down
And watch round yellow turning in the wind.

There's something in the long and awkward stalks
Of sunflowers that is hilarious.

Summer blends its wit with my sea-farm. Funny
Sounds: Bird calls and horses swatting at the flies.
I talk to clover. Is that what is funny?

"Help me to be alive," I say to the sun.
The sun turns its deep spotlight on my sport:
"It's your own life you're riding!"

Las Vegas

My nightclub comedian
Can no longer be found
In the Garden of Eden
Making a call
Across the country to his girl,
Can no longer be seen
In the sauna baths
Where he sat,
A great man
Sweating out his dreams.
He has left his golf course
And deserted his voice teacher,
He's forgotten his elocution lessons
And singing teacher.

His lips
Turn upside down,
His pompadour is gray.
All of his combs
Fall down.
My conceited Happy-go-lucky

Can no longer be found in the Eden Garden
Where he was the great tree and the snake,
And joker, make no mistake, he was Adam and Eve too.

He's on the telephone—Hello? Las Vegas?
Upside-down world,
Glittery old horseshoe world,
Open-door fun palace
Promising stargazing and learning machines,
Gag world open twenty-four hours a day
For mad conversations,
Dream center, mad booth of lemon kings
And roulette-mongers,
Place of winnings and losses,
Wonderland of cactus and roses,
Golden Nugget Singing Eden.

I hear him
Braying in his flat voice:
        I gotta go now.

In My Sleep

The child tells his story.
The ladybug is his friend.
The spirit is his enemy.
The caterpillar eats the moth.
The careers of Barnum and Bailey and the Ringlings
Are depressing the children's government.
The top! The top! He knew it
Would spin forever. Animal acts: He
could tame a flea. Whip
The clown. Frighten the lion
Out of his crib. The life of a cowboy—
Who is that in the saddle?

Winter

The laugh of the comedian
Is a turning point
And the last thing in my mind.

I can't stand
Up to the patter
Of the lonely comedian.

In Manhattan
Snow was forecast by
The radio. But never
Appeared.

The snow will see me out. But
After that——?

More than the snow is falling.
The world's doing pratfalls
And for all I know
Blessings
And bruises are all mixed

Up. I'm breaking up

With the stand-up comedian——
A comedy I seem to confuse
With the end of the world.

"I'm not falling apart,"
I say into the telephone
To the voices that talk back to me,

"But tumbling into a sea

Where I keep my head just
Above water."

EXERCISE: Write a poem about separations.

I have used myself constantly in my own work. The me I first started to write about
was an anxious, frightened person—looking for permanence. I was too "embarrassed"
to say "I'm frightened" or not in touch with myself to say "I am looking for who I am,"
so I used metaphors. The plant metaphor became the symbol of my own search. This is
a poem called "Bitter Sweet"——it was the first poem that I wrote that was published. I
was experimenting by using dialogue in a poem so that other voices were there. What
I wanted to say was "I am looking for permanence"; what I said was "I have found other
flowers"——the flowers became the symbol for what I searched for. The other voices were
all the voices inside my own head.

Bitter Sweet

I

You're allergic said the Mother
It's not my garden said the Aunt
Don't you know rose bushes on public property have thorns
For a reason? The Policeman hemmed and thawed.

The gardener rose and fixed his cap
His hands and face rooted with wrinkles
And seeming soft as earth.
"Well, Missey," he said
"You can plant some parsley behind the lilac bush
And it will grow all winter."
And it did.
Green parsley is still green parsley even in winter;
It doesn't bud, and tastes sour and not green.

II

Downtown in New York City once
In the store about to close,
She bought some opening roses
And clutched them all the way to the hospital.
The tepid nurse composed them by the window
In a vase yellow as the walls and faces.
These faces were replaced by fresher faces.
"Look Daddy! Everyone brings you flowers."
"That's nice" he said, but he didn't notice.

III

Yesterday, beside the jagged wall,
She found a bush with branches dreaming deep
Asleep and twisted, hiding yellow clusters.
She put her naked arm inside the bush
And with struggle pulled away some stalks
Then carried them, triumphant, to the house.
"That's called Bitter-Sweet," he said
And helped her peel the leaves and bottom berries
So she might tuck them in the slender vase.
Peeled faces, sunny red atop the pointed yellow collars
All smile, all day, (nestled in the corner).
Friends say "Though they look like freshest flowers
They dry and last all winter."
But they dry and last forever.

I began writing poems about childhood—because that's when all my "hurt" began. Like a survivor from a holocaust, I had to talk about childhood—the horror of it. I was obsessed with it—and that obsession became a voice.

Normandy Isle

At the age of four on this island I played in the sand
To create twin towers. The jellyfish startled my hand,

But a slippery angel came down to sting at my mind.
I saw one angel crying from a cloud
Change to a sparkling gull, change to a god.
Grief was my angel then; grief that could swim
Under the Christ-fish, over the cherubim.
What angel, what vision, what shrimp hangs in this sky,
Love on its mouth, death in its pure white eye?

EXERCISE: Write about a painful childhood experience.

The World Outside is there for the person who feels deeply to transform. You can take any newspaper event and transform it by your own thoughts. An accident. A separation. A fire. A murder. All of these things act on the imagination. They can be reported or sensed deeply. In poetry nothing real has to happen except the creating of a world. In a novel, play, or nonfiction the weaving thread is a story. And characters. How does one create characters? By listening to how people speak. By observing. By talking with people. Shakespeare wrote, "All the world is a stage," and the writer, "All the world is material." A love affair, a birth, a rejection, a war, a political event—all of this is the outer world to be used. Writing is using the world as material. And the self as the instrument. It's sharpening the senses. Taoist, Zen, and Buddhist philosophies teach us to see "beyond" the shape of things—to get into the essence of events and things. For example, you see a tree moving, but to understand the tree's movement you have to understand the forces of the universe that move it. So, too, in the poem—in the novel—it is not only the world that you look at—inner or outer—but the forces that created the world. Yeats said, "Paint this rhythm not this thing"—it is almost as if all matter has an aura and a rhythm which one enters into as a writer. The writer is both the subject for writing and the invisible prism through which the subject can pass.

Some exercises are helpful for awareness and concentration.

AWARENESS EXERCISES: Examine your body as if you had never seen it before. Look at your hands. Look at your feet.

EXERCISE: Write a body poem.

EXERCISE: Describe the work of an artist in a different medium.

The Work of Nicole Bigar: An Appreciation

Images and alternating currents.
Secrets of the sea. Of loneliness. And the embrace.
Electric in its energies. Strong.
The sheer range of Nicole Bigar's work
Is not a stranger to me.
I have watched her work ripen over the years
And change. Paint. Welding. Styrofoam. Rocks.
All of these materials
Express her private vision.
She is determined to bring innocence and strength
Together. To yolk separates into a whole.
To those who do not expect to find the
Extraordinary—the work of Nicole Bigar is
Shocking. She invents
Again
And
Again
Zoos of feeling
And new forms where the heart
can grow.

A nine-year-old poet responded to my exercise by writing this:

What Makes Me Angry

What makes me angry is when I see fighting
I wish god would strike the two people down with lightning
I see it almost every day
It burns me up when I see too much cruelty
But sometimes I think of people fighting in armor
Colored gold, silver and blue
Fighting is a thing people shouldn't do
Not even in gold, silver or blue

I've got another thing that attracts my mind
Bums
Their minds are always on rum
They've got no home, they sleep in the streets
I have pity on them.

Audrey Butts

EXERCISE: For feelings. How do you really feel about your environment. What does it feel like to be angry?

Pablo Neruda, my friend from Chile, wrote about weariness. It influenced me very much when I was young. It is a weary poem in which a person expresses sadness at injustice.

EXERCISE: Write a poem about being energized.

Joy can also be examined. How do you really feel when you are joyful—how does one feel when one celebrates?

EXERCISE: Write a celebration poem.

A concentration exercise:

The Chinese would often write songs about an ordinary subject. Such as a flower—a lily, for example. The poet, instead of talking about his own emotion, looked carefully at the flower and let the flower speak. A detailed observance became the poem. Write about ordinary things that you have never seen as unusual. Find the beauty in a broomstick.

Here is a poem written about ordinary things in a closet. If you opened your closet, what would you find?

Think of *memories* that clothes evoke.

Opening Up the Closets

On top shelves are round hatboxes
Without hats. Hats on the next shelf.

Beneath the hats are wigs. Hands and faces
On the next shelf down.

What was I called in that dress? I invented
A name that went with the sleeves. Lace
Fans that I wore when I entertained
In ridiculous get-ups. Don't go! The closet's
Not torn down. The shoes below. The shoes
On the heels much too high. Pockets, hems fall. Belts
Are hanging around
Hooks. And a small drawer
Filled with duds.

The next time
Visitors come
I shall invite them to inspect
Our closet. We shall go into my mothball pockets
Finding old letters to mail
And hilarious buttons.

Deep deep into our sleeve-selves
Where the loose stitching falls apart.

EXERCISE: Write a poem about a neighborhood.

Lower East Side in the Alps

Lower East
Side, Tower of Babel, pushcarts,
Temple of last year's newspapers covering
The world in shelters of odor,
Lost house, uncurled palace of broom—
Hair wrapped in curlers and braids,
It is you he feels in this gallery
Where plates hang sterilized, lobotomized

On fresh burlap walls, where penciled lines
Of human faces suffer under glass. It is you,
Tent of string and wash flapping toward
The east of Russia, the west of Vienna, he fears
Bobbing through the ice alps on a train, half insane
To reach the nowhere.
    Beautiful dirt streets,
It is you he walked through in the drawing rooms
Of Paris, where delicate quartets
Played songs of no real Solomon. It is you
He was seeking in the coffins of Greek Islands
(Where everyone sought you), but found
Only red tomatoes walking out of a shoe box. In
The swallowed streets of Chios,
It was you he wanted. It was you in the drugged cafes,
In choked hotels, in mosques, in seas, in the yellow
Peeling bedspreads.

Filth streets, bread-spinning springs of our fathers,
We will sleep in you forever.

Who is the audience?

EXERCISE: Write a poem to someone.

Flesh Song for Children

Consider the Paradise
Consider the sea
Consider the wolf and owl
Consider the thyme
Consider the birdsong and blood
Consider the tree

And laugh
At what has gone wrong.

Writing is about jagged thoughts, streams of consciousness; the mind aloud to daydream and not think conventionally is what writing can be. Everyone says "train the mind" to write. I say "untrain the mind" and be able to imagine. Take risks.

Writing is listening.

I have learned more from Stanislavsky than almost any other teacher. The exercises that he gives to the actor to use the self as the instrument is true of the writer, too. One can "make up" and "create" stories but one "becomes" the characters by borrowing from the self.

Wallace Stevens, insurance executive and poet-extraordinaire, ambassador to the imagination, was one teacher. I learned about poetry from reading Stevens. Perhaps all that one is comes out of the gifts of others—somehow one never forgets one's great teachers. Books were my teachers. I remember first discovering a book by Wallace Stevens. It was blue. I loved the binding. The pages. The physical aspect of the book. Stevens wrote, "The purpose of the poem is to teach you how to write another poem."

How does one begin?
One learns to speak of pain. Of joy. Of colors. One uses the eye to really see. A sculptor said to me yesterday, "I only believe what I see with my own eye." But how many use that iris to see—how many people really look or really listen? Writing is really looking and really listening. Ned Rorem, the composer, said recently, when talking about how he writes music, "By the time I put down music the music is already written. Because the writing takes place before the writing. It takes place constantly in my head. I am always writing." Writing then is being. But being "aware" of one's being as if one was always spying on things. That spying is part of the writing.

Father's Hotel

Give me a mask to hide from your spies, Father,
So I may walk out in my new disguise

Disguised as who I am. But who was I?

They looked at me with such sad, curious eyes,
The elevator boys, and Father's other friends,
Reporting on my movements to my Dad
Who liked to say, "My daughter's all I have,"
As he pressed the bell
And rode from floor to floor of his hotel.

I'm there behind the desk, my suitcase packed,
Leaving for boarding school, behind glass walls
Whispering with sophisticated tact.

Frayed Persian carpets woven in my mind,
The lobby filled with fat, myopic men,
Working for the newly formed U.N.
In turbans, all ignore me as I stand
Apart by all those ashtrays heaped with sand
Waiting to be dropped in my new dress
By an elevator into loneliness.

EXERCISE: Write a poem spying on childhood.

Writing a poem, I sometimes ask "What if?" What Keats called "negative capability"—the possibility of seeing "oneself" in others. His "Ode to a Nightingale" was the poet projecting himself into another's soul.

Opening the senses. Saint Theresa said that a saint is a person who "lives with his senses wide open." That opening up is the preparation for writing.

On this stool
there was a bird
His name was Bateoven
as ever heard. He sang
and ate and drank a
lot. But once he went
through a terrible spot.
He fluttered and gave
us a farewell warning
for he was dead the
next morning.
       Ariel Leve

EXERCISE: Write what it would be like to be a stray animal. What it would be like to be in intensive care. What it would be like to be blind. To be crippled. To be broken in half by loss. To be old. To be a king. To be a dictator.

Here are some poems that eight-year-old and nine-year-old children who studied with me wrote about what it would be like to be a king or queen.

What a Queen and King Do in Spring

Everyone knows that Queens like roses because they are brilliant and gay
But today, on this day of spring, when all flowers bloom
The King joins the Queen in walking through the garden
    looking at the violets and roses.
For on this day of spring, all people like flowers whatever their names
All people like flowers today.
           Adam Casdin

Liza's Visit to the Queen's Garden

Liza took a visit to my garden today
She saw my many flowers
She saw roses and violets
And many other interesting things

At the end of the day
Liza said to me:
"Your garden is so gay.
All the flowers brighten it up.
It doesn't look at all gray."
So I invited her back again to play
With my daughter Jeanna-May.
                    Rhonda Jung

You can research poetry as a journalist. Details are clues to research in poetry. The subject that I picked was construction workers. The noise was so unbearable from beneath my window that my first thought was "I cannot stand it—this noise is keeping me from writing." Then an idea came to me—Hart Crane had written my favorite poem about the Bridge—the building of the Brooklyn Bridge. Of course, it was richer than that. It was about other things also. My thought was—"I will write a poem about construction workers but to understand them I'll go down into the pit with them and understand what they are doing." I put on a hard-hat helmet, and I interviewed construction workers for my poem. I found out the name of their tools, what their demolition machines were called, and their methods of destruction—because these were the demolition people who had the task of getting rid of an old building before a new one could be built. I gathered a glossary of new words—examples—jackhammer, dust machine, bulldozer, gong ball. I asked, "How does this work? Why does this work?" I wanted to know everything. This was a strange world to me—the world of demolition. I sought to understand it without annoying everyone too much. Actually the construction workers were flattered that anyone took such an interest in what they were doing. Here they were destroying buildings all over the city, and no one asked them about their craft. The craft of destruction fascinated me. I spent days talking to these people in their dug-out foundations. Then I decided, quite consciously, what I wanted to write in a poem—the nature of art and destruction. I wanted to liken Gloria Graves, a courageous artist who no one would commission, to the destruction team, who had a purpose and who were well paid. I wanted to make a comment about the artist in society. About Gloria—who destroyed things to create them and was "useless" in the society, who made what she called "constructions" but no one cared about them—and the demolition gang, who made "constructions" but made buildings which were useful. I wanted to talk about both of these people and to make a comparison between them. Almost a mathematical equation. I wanted to write a little bit about Gloria, a little bit about the wreckers, to make a poem that was larger than Gloria or the wreckers—a poem about destruction and construction. Gathering all my facts, I wrote:

Constructions Upper East Side

Wreckers
Drilling and breaking rock
As if New York were one great tooth
Rotten but smiling.
Gloria sits in her studio drilling and breaking boxes.
She is not setting foundations; she is making horses
Talk. She is dis-embalming dolls.
In Manhattan everything is being torn from rock.
Our buildings break. Even the ball,
The gong ball destroying our buildings,
Breaks. Even tools
Built for destruction break.

Outside my window, wreckers
Trapped in constructions: blond
And black men under helmets of steel, caught in earth . . .
Killing earth. The earth is taken somewhere else.
Where does all the earth go?
Wreckers in uniforms of mesh ride
Jackhammers and dust-machines, gripping
Torches of fire. They are precise. Seashells,
The French horn, animal and vegetable are streamlined.

Drills,
The drills sound in my head. I toss words
Back at them. I throw them down as part
Of a new foundation.
I hang words over glass.

Who will escape
This tyranny of the T square?
Gloria, commissioned by
No one, sets up her broken dolls.

Riding past mirrors and new office buildings,
She tries to construct
A small tower out of ivory and horn.
Dreams are nails. Her daydreams ring
On linoleum. Here, the man
Who dropped the bomb on Hiroshima, and went insane,
Grabs back his bomb again.
She's shrinking the jowl and the paunch of Diamond Jim Brady
To clean lines.
Glass is broken.

I borrowed the technique of the construction worker. I wrote. I threw away. I wrote again. I threw away. I wrote the poem perhaps fifty times until I was satisfied, in my own mind, with the rhythms, the language, the research, and with the poem that I built. It was as if I too was a worker, or wrecker, creating my own poem good enough to live in.

EXERCISE: Research a poem by journalistic means. Write about a fire, go to the scene, interview victims, bystanders, firemen.

The reason that people say to me, "When do you write? How do you write?"—they sense that there is a secret. The only secret is feeling that you—as a writer—have something to say. And then the willingness to give priority in time to experimenting and saying it. Not playing a game called "running away" from writing—but actually wanting to write. That *wanting* is the secret.

Most people think that what they have to say is "not interesting" or "not worth saying." They have so many fears about what is interesting that they never try to overcome this lack of confidence. Confidence is what writing is about. It is my own feeling that everybody has something to express that is valuable. What people do not understand is that writing is the *skill* to express anything.

As a writer I cannot assume that I can tell people what to say. But I can truly say that my own life is no more interesting or valuable or important than anyone else's—and out of my own life, my mistakes, my sadnesses, my joys, my confusions, my anger, my bewilderment, my very ordinary things, have come poems, novels, books, articles. Curiosity is part of it. But curiosity can be trained.

The only way I can be a writer is to write. To write as much as possible. To write in my mind when I am not writing on paper. To view everything I do as a "subject" for writing. To view people's lives—the others—as something that will teach me how to live. Writing is expressing what we know about our own lives and what we experienced on earth.

Stories, plots, tales—that is a whole different art. The art of the storyteller usually belongs to the playwright or the novelist. Making up "stories" is a different talent and one that has never really interested me. Basically I am more interested in language and subtleties than I am in action. I could not suggest to anyone how to write a story. But I can suggest how to sharpen one's sensibilities about life, and these sharpened sensibilities can be applied to any kind of writing. The art of observation, of detail, of rhythms of language—these are valuable in any kind of writing.

As poet I have written poetry, which for lack of a term can be called "inner consciousness" or "streams of consciousness." One steps aside from reason and does not interfere with the channel of consciousness that is already inside of one's head. Dream, and poetry of the unconsciousness, both have a logic of their own—an order of their own. The role of the poet is not to interfere with that order but to be an instrument through which these concepts flow. You can call this process "knowing-not knowing" or "nonthinking thinking," which is like saying, "Self-realization is in me—I just have to bring it out." The way I've experienced this is by sitting in front of a typewriter—with paper—and evoking memories or feelings and letting them tumble out. Then, with this raw material in front of me—I try to make an order out of this order. I consciously select from this material a word or an image that leads me to what I want to write about. Then, having told myself about what I want to write, I pick these fragments and write about it.

The Never-Never Man

The Never-Never man swims in my mind
And entertains me. We were once
In an aquarium.

We'd swim around in that exotic pool.
I'd keep him company. Then I'd go home.
He swam to me over the telephone. Asked
Me to come back into the pool. At that time
I was young. A butterball.

That's all clear as crystal. What I don't understand
Is why Never-Never dangles in my mind.
Zip up the lid. Wonder about the book.
Picture him now: Poor lost
Fish. It's the mind
That keeps me indifferent. I cannot explain.
The Never-Never man was at least his own ghost.
Swim back to me.
Sealed behind glass, he
Whispers, "Never-Never."

EXERCISE: Write, without thinking, about an experience. Let the words come out whatever way they will. Try not to hold back any thought, positive or negative, and to even use bizarre words and images if you feel like it.

In an odd way I have reached "transcendence" through writing. And I have stayed "sane" by writing. Writing has given me a "way" to live my life, to go beyond the personal self into another world where real life ends and fantasy takes over—a world of letters where the symbolic action becomes you—the poem or novel is you—and you shed "yourself" of "yourself"—you create, in another way, another "You." A better "You" that does not change. A book that can travel around the world, be in the "hands" of others—a kind of shadowbox that has your soul and your thoughts in it—without being your body. Your bloodstream is not in the words on paper. And, yet, without You and your bloodstream, without the blood that ran through the arteries, without the mind pumping imagination into that odd chamber of the watery brain where thought is born and takes place—that other "You" would not exist to multiply you and be your "seed" which travels around the universe and through time into infinity. Without You the product of the poem or song or novel or exposé could not be. Behind Hamlet was a person imagining Hamlet and scribbling into alphabet signs, or the symbolic action of thought, language; this person's "thought" which could be acted out a million million times throughout eternity as long as the English language survives. Without a person training himself to commit that act—to write—there would not be the being that is *able* to open up. Opening up. To a new part of oneself. That is part of being "a writer."

Writing has a life on earth. Books, like humans, have lives. That is why "creating" is a holy process to me. I suppose I write because it is the only way I know of to defeat death. Each day I become aware of "getting older" and losing "my body" and "my looks." It is to writing that I turn for a better mirror. In my books I see another person reflected. The powerful me. The foolish me. The jester in me. For writing is a kind of power. A kind of force. A force that does not kill.

The Problem of David

He lay with his head filled with psalms
Wondering how a boy
Could shed all dreams from his mind
And arise to conquer a giant.
The battle was set for dawn.
All the dark night he lay,
Facing the stars and his God
Without a plan. Visions, am I to die?
My mind is caught with the tunes
You taught me when I was a child.
They will not let me arm.
How shall I begin
To think of the battle, the way
To fight my enemy?
Only these songs remain
To keep me company.
When the army was all arrayed,
And Goliath stood in that place
Where he knew the battle would be,
David, armed for the moment of death,
Turned all songs to a stone
And overthrew the flesh.

EXERCISE: Write a poem about defeat. About conquering.

Writing is a seduction. A seduction of the reader. "Come into me" I say with my body—lying down on my bed—my legs spread—my lips parted for love. That feeling good—being filled—is what the writing process is also. "Read me" or "Hear me" or

"Open me" is what we say. No one has ever been rejected by writing a book. The book may be "rejected" but the writer is intact.

I mention all this to show that the "subject" of poems for me comes in clusters. It is a period of twenty years that I have been publishing poems (my first poem won an award from *New World Writing* and was published when I was seventeen) and my first book published in Paris when I was twenty. These twenty years have seen contradictions, growth, change, and hopefully a craft learned. It has been, so far, a "life" of poetry— poetry being the breath and food of my existence.

I do not recommend writing poetry constantly. I like to vary writing poems with creating films, writing plays, writing journalism, writing novels—the whole spectrum of writing interests me. Whatever I learn from one discipline I pour back into the writing of poetry.

A secret for me is involved with health. I like to play tennis, not to drink too much, to stay "fit" in order to write well. I think of all the romantic visions of nineteenth-century romanticism where poets were obliged to drink themselves to death or to die tragically, like Rimbaud, or Raymond Radiguet, or Keats or Shelley. I think that health is important for me to survive and that poetry is another form of health. I think of myself as an athlete of the imagination. Every day I try to run the distance.

What to write about?
Everything is a subject for poetry. I learned this from Marianne Moore, who could write about brooms. And from Elizabeth Bishop, who showed me poems about sardine factories.

All writing is written in the mind," says English tabloid journalist Robin Leach. "Writing requires discipline. When you are writing, sitting in front of a typewriter is worse than being a prisoner in a cell. You must padlock a large ball and chain to the front of you so you don't move away. For poets, writing is a cleansing of the soul. Wouldn't you say so? That's what *real* writers do. Not me. I don't write. I report. You, Sandra, say that writing is a beautiful thing to do. I think it's the most painful preoccupation and profession in the world. In my business (writing for breezy tabloids—the Murdoch chain and others) I can tear up twenty sheets of paper just to get the first paragraph correct."

EXERCISE: Write a tabloid poem. Buy or borrow a yellow paper and take the same subject matter—"Boy Murdered by Chicken" or something similar—and create a poem about it. Go subject searching.

Robin Leach goes on to say, "Writing is a beautiful pain in the ass." Writing is something you do with your body as well as your brain. The question is: How do you get it out of your body where it is beautiful (in your own head) and out on the paper to the readers? That's where the pain is. (I became a writer because I like to talk to people, you know.)

EXERCISE: Write a poem that is a conversation with others.

Patience is necessary, the necessary craft of a writer. In his correspondence on aesthetics, Gustave Flaubert wrote, "Until now you have only lacked patience. I do not think that patience and genius are necessarily one, but at times patience is the sign of genius and takes its place."

Flaubert also wrote: "One must produce art then for oneself alone—as one plays the violin. Musset will remain by the side of him whom he disowns—he has beautiful gushes, beautiful outbursts, that is all; but the Parisian in his character hinders the poet, his dandyism vitiates his style, his knees are stiff from the tautness of his garters, the 'powers' for becoming a poet are lacking; he has thought neither of himself nor of his art, but of his passions. He has solemnized (with undue emphasis) the heart, the feelings, love . . . to the depreciation of the highest perfections . . . the heart alone is the poet," etc. "This kind of thing flatters women; convenient maxims which make so many people believe themselves to be poets without knowing how to produce a line of poetry. The glorification of the mediocre exasperates me. It is a denial of all art, of all beauty; it is an insult to God's aristocracy."

More from Flaubert: "The secret of a work of art then, is to be found in the agreement of the subject matter with the temperament of the author."

EXERCISE: Describe the most unusual person that has passed your way.

For me it was a bizarre madman that I saw in the streets of Nepal. He was walking the streets calmly and I began hearing the words "love singer" in my mind. I didn't know what "love singer" meant but I allowed myself to go back to the hotel where I was living and just write down whatever came into my mind about that person. I wrote the poem, "The Love Singer" (which later became the basis for a musical play, *The Life Singer*).

The Love Singer

He appeared
Without a shadow,
Crying joy in a language that
We had forgotten or never knew
As syllables dropped like kumquats
From his tongue and he smiled at boys
In the street who made fun of him. He
Did not seem "Western"——he was too mad for
That, jangled and put together in a shabby way
That might have embarrassed us. And from
What place in the East he had arrived we could
Not tell——he seemed to have shed his origin
The way flowers shed petals
Until only the stem remains. And he was
That stem. Thin, made of sunlight, his face burned
By wind (all the streets he had been to!),
And he wandered
Past gaps, white buildings,
Glassy windows bursting with
Jewelry, past flowers,
Mirrors——
And what he sang was again this word joy,
Sounding so much like a bird
Calling to his invisible mate
As he flies beyond the New Territories,
Then dips into a mountain.

Love Singer! Perhaps he once played at being
A bard in China before
Singing

In our parking lots, gardens, traffic, new
Hotel lobbies. And we listened.
And I keep asking,
"What is his name?" and
"What does he sing?" and
"What do you call that stringed
Instrument, which seems to be cared for and polished
By feathers?" Here
In this city,
Every day we have seen this miracle-monger
Walking the streets. But only once
Did I hear him speak to me clearly.

Cocteau wrote, "I love the unwearying charm of mingled civilizations. A buddha with Greek torso and curls."

I have published six books of poetry. My favorite book is *Love Letters from Asia*, where I enter the world of Buddha and Thailand.

Visiting Buddha

Outside

Walking around. The temple,
Quiet as a hospital.

I wanted to make a shuffling
Sound with my feet. I wanted to find
My shoulders. I wanted to look
At my toes—more than that,

Get strangers to walk with me.

I wanted to make clicking noises
Into the faces of unknown stockings and shoes,

And I wanted
To make short circles with my feet.

Inside

The stupas are curling as mad
As ice cream,
And the long, golden Buddha
Is candy king
In this temple.

In this temple of candy
The long, sleeping Buddha reclines. He's
thinking of nothing. He's longer
Than any god. His toes

Take up the entire
Lower temple.

Always the dreamer is lost
As if he must be, to please us,
A blown-up balloon. Now

The shrimp priests
Bow to the giant's toe

And compare their own
Size to his. Why did they build the temple
Around the king?
They should have let him sleep in
The street near the trees.

EXERCISE: Write a poem in which a statue comes alive.

It is true that in different times of my life I have been concerned with different subjects and I always centered on these subjects—went with them—and allowed myself to listen to myself to "hear" what it was I wanted to write myself out of—what obsession was inside of me. My earliest poems, written from the age of eight to about the age of twenty, were almost all about my own life, my parents and childhood. My first poem appeared in Cherry Lawn School in the yearbook, *The Cherry Pit*. It was about loneliness and winter. Later, I went to Bennington College where I majored in "writing." It was an ideal time because there were many tutors of poetry—excellent poets teaching literature and working in a tutorial way with young writers. I studied in a tutorial with Howard Nemerov, Ben Bellit, Kenneth Burke, and Francis Golffing. Each teacher opened my mind to a new concept. Nemerov to the importance of using one's own life as a subject matter for poetry. "It all begins in the home," he said. (That's probably the reason behind the title of my first book, *Voyage Home*.) The first book that I wrote after I left college was *Manhattan Pastures*. Just as *Voyage Home* (which had been published in Paris by Anaïs Nin and Lawrence Durrell) dealt with childhood, fairy tales, and myths about one's own life, *Manhattan Pastures* had a definite subject matter—the subject of the city. *Manhattan Pastures* won the Yale Younger Poets award and I had the opportunity of working with the fantastically amusing, erudite, and charming editor Dudley Fitts (who died in 1968). Fitts was a classical scholar and also had a great sense of humor. He called me "Bardolino" after the wine we drank together and encouraged me to write poems that were sensual and bizarre.

My next book was written several years later. It was called *The Vaudeville Marriage,* and just as *Voyage Home* dealt with the subject matter of childhood, and *Manhattan Pastures* with the experience of being isolated in the city—and the great urban nightmare— The Vaudeville Marriage dealt with relationships. The main poem was based on a very personal experience—a relationship I had for two years with a comedian. But beyond my own "relationship" it dealt with the whole buffoonery of trying to make pocketbooks out of pigs' ears and princes out of paupers and ideal relationships out of personalities doomed to conflict with each other.

Love Letters from Asia is the exact opposite of confessional poetry. It was written after the shocking news of Sylvia Plath's suicide. I was so depressed by the death of America's most gifted poet that I decided to write a book that would be the other side of the moon to Ariel—a book that would only praise and celebrate. Written almost in memoriam to Anne Sexton. *Love Letters from Asia* was a book only on the theme of contentment and love. It was followed by *Maps for the Skin* (published as a section in selected poems, *Earthworks*), a book about a person whose life is beginning to go to seed. Also a book about earth and its value.

The theme of the next book, *Futures*, was the theme of the secrets of anxiety and the screams of women. I have waited five years for the next collection of poems, called *Songs to Love and Age*.

Who stepped on you?
Who hurt you?
What are you left out of? Why?
Does your sex or race have anything to do with this?
Does your poverty? your wealth?
Are you where you want to be?

EXERCISE: Complain through your poems. Howl. Scream. Lament. Let go. Use the poem as a hospital in which you can be cured. Get the sickness inside of you out.

Bleeding

In bed my life has started bleeding again.
Out of my pores, out of the strange sun-pores of blood
Come mother and father warning me not to be a
Wise-guy. Out of my pores come all the teachers who
Made me hate reading and writing—and suddenly out of
My body come the merciless men who took my
Eyes and lips and body—my first husband playing the violin
Spills out of my skin—I no longer can rest with him
Putting my face under the security of his blond hair
Which came out of his arm—there
Are the other monsters there—the poet who turned out
To be berserk, the comedian-jerk, the pilot who lied,
The strange blue-eyed Italian boy who drove with me through
Scotland, and the husband who could not like me. I am
Bleeding now too much. Take a mop.
All this blood shall be clotting on the bed. There is
No one here
Giving my signs away, my secrets stay with me, but
The albumen comes out, with legs of dead loves
That begin to clot.

Walking the Walls

As I am following my
Toes up the wall, I know that another place exists,
Somewhere else, where women, for example,
Are not climbing the walls. In another
Place palm trees bend in the sun—the green
Joints of the great sensual palms open their
Fronds, paradise in the palms, opening
Like hands. People I do not remember
Wait to welcome me. They identify me
As the woman who always carries a picture
Of her daughter next to her hat or her
Heart. I am often found
Waiting to go back
To the Center of the Earth, the hollow earth,
I know it is there, by all that is true,
I know it is there—beyond snow—
A place where children play, where people
Are not afraid of affection, where there
Is order and no fear of time. The Center of
The Earth is there for those who know
That kindness is everything, and love
Doesn't have to be scarce as uranium. Anyway,
I'm up on the walls today
Like an upside-down tiger, looking at walls,
Staring at them under my feet,
As always, writing pictures that resemble
Screams, as always writing a documentary
On loneliness, shooting it all in my head—
The whole asylum that is here in your papers—
Shooting it all in my head—the documentary
Writing—on the walls.

The Chinese poets were ordinary men in the times of the Tang dynasty who actually wrote about simple things. They wrote about the way of life in rhythms and beautiful language. Their poetry was historical—it centered on events—unusual and ordinary—on nature, on romance, on the earth and human condition. Chinese poetry was written to be read. To be verbalized between friends. The poets were the entertainers. Without our modern communications of radios, television, cassettes, satellites, the poet was the bard who spoke about the way of life, poems being the exaggerated and often beautiful commentary on life.

Conversation of Poets

That was China! Where blue
Tiles spanned half the world—blue
Feathers hammered
By the sun. Poets wise
As Solomon
Whispering in the gardens,
Walking between gold pebbles,
Quiet, joyful, practical men.
Not one of them could be labeled mad.
All in another lifetime,
Great marble lions chiseled
And refined by water. I envy
Those poets—not their king. He
Was another thing—as we can
Imagine—seeing the broken
Columns of his city and
His clothes,
Now strands of dust sealed
Inside museums. They said,
In those days, "Poets
Are our kings—we'll bury
Them in tombs larger
Than homes!"

I envy their affection,
Brilliant as colors,
Their light-headed kindness
To each other. They took
Long walks and held each
Other, fingers clasped in the open gardens.
In their gardens
They exchanged new songs
And secrets.
Time was on their side

Today our commentators, newscasters, commercials, have replaced our poets. Our meditations are brought to us by sponsors. And yet—to be sane—we can backtrack to the traditions of human voices waiting to be reheard. The Tang poet—in each of us—is locked in the mind, waiting to get out. Our habits of dreams, our disobedient souls, our horrified sense of justice, our longings, fears, angers, follies, and jokes, are all there—waiting for the outlet—the word and behind the word the voice, which we commit to paper in a poem.

While teaching a young poets' workshop I ask children to write memos to themselves—a poetry exists in lists. Nothing is too unimportant for a poem. A poem—for me—is everything—a map of the skin, a silence made real, a way of using the eye, of looking at lists and changing them into song. Memos are jottings, seamarks, shorthand. A memo is a good way to begin. One is afraid of the word "poem" but not afraid of the word "memo." The main thing in poetry writing is not to be afraid and to desanctify the overwhelming task of writing. If you say, "I have to have a great idea to write a poem," the magical spontaneity that is part of writing freezes inside the gut. However, if one starts with jottings, ideas, lists, personal thoughts of oneself, the writing becomes an easier second nature.

EXERCISE: Write a poem about a separation. Imagine having to return objects.

For me writing has been a way of living.
A personal catharsis in oneself.
And, on another level, a way of fixing moments, of keeping an imaginative history of one's life and what one sees and thinks.

On another level, poetry is a way of centering oneself. A perpetual reporting of the mind to the paper—an exercise not unlike the new-way exercises of t'ai chi ch'uan.

Writing, like dance, exercises must be done again and again and again every day.

Keeping the body healthy is part of keeping the mind in tune also.

The spirit of the writer becomes the spirit of the work.

Rhythms. Sensitivity. Feeling. Intelligence. An ability to take risks. The discovery of feelings is a voyage the writer must undertake. Feelings about nature. The whole world of nature is a subject for poetry. Imagine entering into the souls of animals, minerals, objects.

Nothing is too small to be written about. Open one's senses to what it means to be a giant. Just as a painter sketches small objects and large, the poet can tune his energies to enormous masses and small masses of what is living. Study a book on the stars. Write about the planets—Venus, Mercury, Jupiter. Gather the solar vocabularies. Then write poems on insects. Look in an insect book. For me, opening a book on insects, I read, "What strikes us most about insects must surely be their energy, especially the persistence by which they apply it. Nothing like this is to be found anywhere in the animal kingdom. The pestering fly in sunshine and the blood sucking mosquito at night are examples known to us all. The industry of the ant and the bee is another form of it." Become entomologists of the imagination. A study of insects, of their external structure, of their eyes, of their glands, of their production of sound, of their coloration, of their classification and nomenclature, of their interdependencies and metamorphosis, will teach you about poetry. Scientific accuracy is indispensable to the poet's craft. It is helpful to get in touch with a subject—by studying it.

Once one is aware of the silk glands', the poison glands', the wax glands', and the scent glands' work, one has the material from which one can work an intricate poem. Details are everything. From details to feeling.

Details are the essence of what is interesting.

Feeling is then observing very carefully. To allow oneself the luxury of knowing unimportant details—to be a scholar of everything—is the poet's condition.

Marianne Moore was perhaps one of the American poets who showed that imagination, detail, and the world outside are part of the poet's handbook. Reason creates and imagination enlarges.

Getting in touch with oneself, one's feelings, one's history, and one's own feelings about the world leads to poetry. For Wallace Stevens it was the poetry about order and disorder—the poet as the high priest of the invisible. For Mao Tse-tung it was poetry that had to act as aesthetic teaching and a catalyst to action. Two different poets—living at the same time—both philosophers going against the grain. Wallace Stevens lived in Hartford, Connecticut. He went to work every day as an executive of an insurance company. He said, "There must be something of the peasant in every poet." And also that "poetry is a statement of a relationship between a person and the world."

Mao Tse-tung was a peasant poet who grew to manhood in Hunan, China, and became a teacher. Because of the political upheaval in China, he was directed into a political career and into political poetry which reflected his thoughts on the world. His poetry was a way of revolutionizing the masses by putting his beliefs and inspirations simply. Poetry here is seen as revelation.

Allen Ginsberg changed American political thinking by showing, through his handbook, *Howl*, that living loose was okay. Ginsberg, along with Gary Snyder, who is deeply involved in Chinese and Japanese meditation and thought, borrowed insight from the East, consciousness, and cool. Ginsberg mixed the black anger of our ghettos, the outrage of the outsiders, to a technological system where nothing had meaning and stimulated passions with his poetry. Ginsberg and marijuana created the sixties in America. The power of Ginsberg's poetry was the passions of a disenfranchised, nonliterary group of young people who would never "make it" in the system. Daring to call the emperor's clothes, they invented their own counterculture system, which was the invention of the beat generation. The beatitudes (beat from beatitudes) of these people were expressed in "Howl," "Kaddish," and the quieter haiku of Gary Snyder—as well as the questioning political poems of Rexroth, Levertov, and Ferlinghetti. Injustice was the subject, passion was the agent, and anger was the force. These poems questioned modern science, modern industry, modern society. The feelings of anger in the poetry became the energy on which the counterculture was founded.

EXERCISE: What angers you?

We often experience while reading novels or poems—that's "how I feel." Literature is a way of getting in touch with someone else. We have to be in touch with our own self to get in touch with others.

In touch with our age. Our anger. Our ripeness. Our vulnerability. The confessional poem is no more than telling of secrets. Getting in touch with the past and spilling out the good or bad experiences. When one talks to a "confessor" or a "doctor," one is not supposed to hold anything back. Imagine that the paper is this confessor. Tell deepest secrets. Do not be afraid.

Do not be afraid is the essence of getting in touch with oneself. Afraid of what?

Afraid of what?
Phony poastic bone,
Drops of sound dumb as tympanum,
White ear doldrum down
In luxurious whispers of secret
Adulteries,
Long-distance confessions
Of friendship and mystery voices
Announcing the time or again
And again "Do not be

Afraid." How else will she
Comfort me——her voice curling
Alphabets? And to whom
Do I press my lips
Zipping haystack kisses
And telling of my latest poem?

Wait a minute. They are
Beating a woman. Do not be afraid,
I wish to inform her
Through my telephone.
Hello? Cannibal? Goddess? I am home,
Minister, Prophet, Murderer, Madam,
Your loss of sensitivity's in my ear.

EXERCISE: Write a poem about fear.

Getting in touch with yourself does not mean controlling your thoughts. It means the opposite—letting all the thoughts come into you and then selecting them.

While teaching poetry to children at the Metropolitan Museum in an effort to open young minds to the wonders of the outer and inner self, I held a class in the Greek vase room. A tennis instructor called Byron Sanders came to speak about the body in Greek culture. He spoke about the athletic games in which people worshiped the body. Through his power the hero could do anything.

EXERCISE: Write about a hero.

Using a museum is one way to open the mind to concepts for poems.

EXERCISE: Go to a museum. Go to the collection of art and write about ordinary things.

Discover how ordinary things connect to the inner life.

EXERCISE: Go to the ancient section and write poems about the body, allowing the sculptures and ideals of the senses to inspire the poem. As Keats wrote "Ode to a Grecian Urn," we can also be inspired by the history intact in works of art.

In the *Iliad* or *The Poem of Force*, Simone Weil talks about the true hero, the true subject of the Iliad is force. The essence of Homer was not only a description of the wars (Homer wrote epic poetry—powerful poetry which described historical events—as opposed to lyrical poetry, which aims at only describing particles of human feeling). But the epic that Homer wrote was concerned not only with destiny and force—but the extent to which the soul creates its own destiny. Homer is the great historian of his time. Poetry is a form of history. Homer is said to have been blind, but it is possible that the blindness of Homer is only a *symbolic* taking out of the cold brutality of the body and the mind twisted.

Modern epic poetry deals with the mind gone wrong and the body twisted. Here are some of the poems written by my young students about anger:

Instructions

Stop talking!
Sit down!
Listen to your teacher!
Have respect!
Go to bed!
Take the dog out!
Do your homework!
Study!
Fold flap A under flap C
And twist knob B
End!

Amanda Green

My Brother Makes Me Angry

My brother makes me angry every day
Early in the morning we always start a fight
At night while eating dinner he has to get me
Into trouble
My brother always gets on my nerves
When I tell him to do something
He never does it
My brother makes me angry!

Nicole Smith

That Makes Me Mad

I love my brother and I always will
But once in a while, well more than that
I feel like a serf the way my mother
Bosses me around and tells me to get things
For my brother.
He is younger than I am and that makes it

Worse.
My mother is always saying,
"You have to set a good example for
Your little brother"
She always blames me if something bad
Happens
And that makes me mad!

Lonny Fredericks

Another way that the poet enters the domain of the senses is through fairy tale and imagination. The once upon a time of the ideal world—the ideal as being able to be reached through the voyage of suffering of the poet. Here the poet becomes the seer, the mystic in the woods, traveling through suffering—a sacrificing person—the accent being on human misery as a precondition for revelation.

Dante, who was a political outcast, living in the city of Florence in the late thirteenth century, was exiled from his city because of the war between two factions of power—the Guelfs and the Ghibellines. Dante, pursued, lived in a temporary shelter outside of his city and wrote his vision of man striving from Inferno through Purgatorio to Paradiso. In this epic Dante also wrote of a person's love of a place. Florence, the city itself, was also his beloved. Beatrice, a vision of a woman, became the ideal. Dante went with his teacher into Inferno (the historical past) which mixed his own friends with mythical and historical people—all paying for their "sins" by physically embodying the sins themselves. With his teacher, Virgil, he travels from ignorance to understanding, to revelation—the hell, purgatory, and heaven of the senses. On one level Dante is teaching us how to write a poem. That voyage from pain into memory, through understanding, and then to higher wisdom, is the voyage that everyone experiences in reaching understanding. Paradise is the end of understanding.

Opening the mind to the world now, one can write one's own epic.

EXERCISE: Feelings on the war in Vietnam. Feelings on the massacre at the Olympics. Feelings on the assassination of Robert Kennedy.

Separation is an experience—the hello and good-byes of life—that touches our deepest feelings. The separation of umbilical cords—real or imagined—the separation that comes with death, divorce, the end of a love, the end of things—are all explosive subjects which allow us to enter our map of feelings.

EXERCISE: Write a poem on your own separations in childhood, schools, war, loves, jobs, all of the experiences that have joined you or unjoined you with life.

I have spent the past twenty years of my life teaching—you cannot really teach people how to write (any more than you can teach people how to lead their lives), and yet I firmly believe that a teacher can create the *atmosphere* in which people become less afraid of writing, believe in what they have locked inside themselves, and are stimulated to go inside themselves to write.

Because anyone can write who has the will to write—to overcome the fear. Language, like breath, is inside everyone. Musicality is inside all of us—it's a question of learning the discipline of writing by making it no discipline at all. *One has oneself as one's own instrument*, I learned from acting. Writing is like acting in the sense that it is an acting out—but it is an acting out symbolically. You release fear, you *release* magic, you create characters, situations, moods, insights, revelations, and other worlds by going *inside* yourself. There are worlds inside oneself. Words are the key. Not being afraid is also the key. Not being afraid to take the "particularities" (another word used often by Stanislavsky in acting) and writing them down.

Two years ago I started a young poets' workshop for children at the Hewitt School. With seven-year-olds I pretended that the paper I gave them was their "magic book" and the pens I gave them were "magic pencils" (all writing materials are "magical" to me). Then I asked the children not to be afraid of writing and asked them, during the year, to write about different situations.

I asked the children to write about what poetry is. (The main thing was not to "worry" about spelling and not to "worry" about rhyme. I explained that there were many patterns of rhyme—called prosody—including the sonnet, the sestina, the rondel, etc., but that was a question of learning a form, which we could do later. I asked them to use rhyme whenever they felt like it—whenever it felt natural and made them feel good. That a rhyme helped a poet by giving them a way *into* thoughts—to go with the rhymes which were words that matched sounds—that they might not already have. Rhymes are ways of creating divine *accidents* and are a help to the streams of the subconsciousness, but do not always have to be used. My main thought was to give the children the courage to be simple, the courage to be nonsensical, and the courage to use humor and feeling.) Here is a poem written by a young poet on poetry:

Poetry

Potre is nice while you are skating on ice.
Or it can be fun while sitting in the sun.
Or you can do potre here or there
Or you can do it anywear.
Potre you can do it in class
Or in your bath
Make your potre good
So it looks like a hood.
When ever you have the time
Sit down and make your potre rimes.
                    Didi Dreher

Poems have music in them, I explained. But a nice subject to write about is music itself. I helped the children by writing a few vocabulary words on the blackboard. To pick out "special" words before writing a poem is always useful. The words I remember giving were

Guitar

Sitar

Drums

Here is a poem written by a young poet on music:

Music

I will drum for my mum,
And I might for my brother Mike.

I will sitar for my sister,
Guitar for my father.
Samantha Phillips

I explained that William Blake was one of my favorite poets. He lived at the beginning of the Industrial Revolution in England—in the nineteenth century when things made by "hands" were being replaced by things made by "machines." Blake saw a loss of innocence happening to the world all around him—by people becoming "numbers" in factories and not being craftsmen or craftswomen anymore and giving up their lives to work in coal factories and cotton factories where the world was becoming less personal. Poetry is a return to the "personal" and making a poem is a craft of innocence. I also showed how Blake illustrated his manuscripts with drawings—a way of making the poem even more "beautiful" and "crafted." I encouraged the young poets to create drawings on their poems. And to write about personal things. Here is an exercise that I created—to WRITE ABOUT LOVE—what love sounds like, how love moves, what love is specifically to you. Here is a response to this exercise:

Love Is

Love is a violin that plays so pretty
  Love is a kiss just like a flute.
    Love is a marriage with a piano.
    Love is a nice note to hear.
      Love is a good friend.
        Love is a dancer.
          Love is a singer.
            Love is the famous Beethoven.
          Love is a man
            And a woman with a nice feeling.

Cara Williams

Poetry can encompass all feelings, dreams, fantasies. Inside of us are WISHES which can't get out—life-secrets. Writing a poem is often like telling a secret to a very good friend. The paper becomes the friend. Writing about wishes can be an exercise:

My Wish

If everyone could get together,
And clean up the city,
It would take a long, long time.
It would be simple,
But we would have to split up.
We could clean the windows,
Stop throwing things around,
And most of all,
Stop polluting the water and air.
When it was finished we would see to it
That nobody threw trash on the streets.
They would have to stop smoking
And soda cans and leftover foods
Would be in the garbage can.
Suzanna Fairchild

TELL ME ALL ABOUT YOURSELF, I would say to my young poets. And I created the exercise for young poets about telling life-secrets. But it's not only for young people—it's the exercise I muse upon and most often use myself when I sit down in front of my big bold IBM typewriter and don't know what to write. (I like to write on a typewriter because the poem comes out in print.) WRITING SECRETS is one of the best exercises I know of for poets—young and old.

Me, Myself, and I

I really like to run.
   I think it's very fun.
      One of my secrets is—
            I like to be a pig doing a jig.
         I love my mommy.
               She is charming—not too vain.
               But my sister is a pain.
               I want it to rain.

I call my sister Murtle,
But she really is not a turttle.

Kiwesa King

Secrets of Kim

Glittery springs of water shining like crystals.
Look like shiny water pistols.
Shining crystal clear.
Ice is melting,
Water can't.
And water grows a water plant.
There is one thing ice can't do.
It can't give warmth—
Neither can you.

Kim Sais

EXERCISE: Write a poem that is a secret.

Another exercise that I use myself when I want to write a poem but am not sure about what I want to write is to write about imaginary places. The sound and odor of them. To WRITE ABOUT A PLACE is a miraculous exercise—suddenly you are transported there and are re-creating an environment—imaginary and real. Here are two poems I have written about places—and one written by my daughter and young poetry student Ariel about an imaginary place. My places are Guadeloupe and Hong Kong. Her place is Candyland.

Places

Sorrow has made of my world a new condition
Imagine living in a useless island where tea is
Good, the wine is from Portugal, and the main
Church has only a front facade like a piece from

A play——scenery——the back of the church is gone.
I remember visiting Macao. The pedicabs were driven
Aimlessly——old men riding bicycles and taking
Tourists to the fan-tan parlors. There——on the ships——
You could hear the long nights of mah-jongg and gambling
Cards. I went there, wondering what it would be like
To never come back. To hide, for example,
In a small factory where girls attached beads to sweaters,
To duck beneath that table of small stones, never to
Come out. Or slip
Into the cracks of an ancient wooden building where once
Portuguese martinets held their parties and their drills. What
Would it be like, to never leave, to suddenly be lost
In the gambling place where baskets were lowered over heads,
Never to be heard of again?

In St. Thomas, dancing
At a ball given
For the Arts Association where men
In strange headdresses dance with me——who am I?
Where women await the giving of the door prize, I dance
With a pharmacist in red velvet pants
And plastic see-through vest. His black skin
Is moving to the beat, while he admits
His greatest accomplishment is a collection of
Mistresses and a wardrobe of fancy shoes. Who am I
Walking in Macao? Who was I in
Chios looking for a place to inconspicuously go to the
Bathroom without being noticed by a monk? Or
Driving down the Keys——the Florida mangroves
On each side of me? What am I doing in Paris
Where I hunt for masks in the Museum of Man? Or in Belgium
Shoved by tourists marching like blown-up animals in the
Macy Parade?
The desire to disappear, the desire to rid myself of my life——

All of this leads me to places, where, for moments,
I lose the stuff of legs and arms and hair and history
That has carried me everywhere before.

My Trip to Candyland

I'm on my way to Candyland
Where all the candy canes are green,
And everything must be seen.
I fly up and over the clouds
And I fly over deserts which have lots of sand
And I fly over places where washing clothes are clinging.
And finly I land
And everything is black
And then I look
And see that it is night.

Ariel Leve

The poet is an *inner historian* taking X rays of history, by revealing the insides of human beings' souls. Homer showed in the *Iliad* and the *Odyssey*, which recorded the wars of Troy, how frail humans were transformed by merciless necessity to suit their own fate which was determined by the gods. Homer showed through his epics, as the Greeks showed through all their tragedy, how human beings are brought down by shame, lust, pride, all of the forces that can ruin a life.

EXERCISE: Create an exercise on the abstractions of force. Write poems on hatred, pride, shame, content, insufferable indifference, misfortune.

The Greeks, like Homer, were endowed with spiritual forces which enabled them to try to avoid or at least be aware of self-deception. Freud, and his legacy of analysis and self-analysis, enables us to be heroes by giving us the tools of self-knowledge. Telling the truth about one's own life has influenced modern poetry—particularly the modern poets whom we call confessional. Confessional poetry was taken to extremes by Robert Lowell.

126

On first hearing Robert Lowell and reading his work, I was transformed by his poetry—by the use of religious imagery, confessional details, and by the fact that many of his poems were "for" people. Poems for the Union dead, poems for the dead religious fanatic Jonathan Edwards, poems for his mother, his friends. Later, as I kept learning to write by trial and error (learning about poetry by writing poetry) I began writing poems FOR PEOPLE as an exercise. Perhaps the ones that I like the best are the poems I wrote, while pregnant, for my unborn child. It was so real—to have a child inside my stomach, floating around in water, and to have through all the watery passages of my brain conceptions of that stranger that would—soon—be the "closest" person to me. Also, since I had been an only child and always lived away from a "family," growing up "alone" in boarding school, the fact of creating a "family" was awesome. These are the poems I wrote for my unborn child. (One might take the exercise of writing poems for people you know. A whole collection was recently made by Erica Jong called *Mashnotes for the Dead*. Remember if you follow this exercise that poems can be written for heroes or heroines, people alive or dead, kings or convicts, officials or bums.)

My daughter Ariel, now nine, once asked me, "What was the first poem you ever wrote?" I thought about it and couldn't remember, since I think I began writing notes to myself about things when I was seven or eight—only no one noticed them or cared and they were not called "poems"—words that are lost. But I do remember being a freshman at Bennington College and my poet-teacher (and hero—oh! I wanted to be a poet just like him) Howard Nemerov said to me that he had submitted my poem "Silence" (about seagulls) to New World Writing (then an important literary magazine and the first American literary magazine to be in the paperback format and sold on newsstands and in airports). When my poem was selected by the judge—Philip Boothe—and I saw my name in print for the first time, I carried the poem around with me everywhere. My first poem in print! It was like a certificate to myself of myself. When others told me they "read it" (meaning they "read inside me"), I felt as if I had made an X ray of myself public to the universe. I loved seeing my poem in print and was very encouraged by this. (Which is why I encourage my students to publish their poems as soon as they can.) Here is the poem, which was the first one I saw in print:

Silence

One moment before flight, the seagulls long
To trade their perfect movement, and
I, in childhood, pitied them.

Salt tears cripple the wind. I walk
This standard island where mechanics rule
Dreams on an empty stencil. How we long
For movement in this landscape.

And here is a poem (even more beautiful, I think) that my daughter Ariel had written (before she ever read mine) on the same subject of the seagull:

Drifting

Soft and swift comes the seagull
Spreading his wings over the beach.
He russels through the wind
Like a pencil on paper
As he flys over the ocean
Into the sky.

Ariel Leve

What to write about? There is the whole world—the world of secrets, places, animal, vegetable, mineral. Two exercises that work very well are to write a poem about JEWELS and a poem about ANIMALS. When I asked the young poets to write about jewels, we talked about the different stones and I made a glossary of words:

Emeralds

Rubies

Silver

Gold

Here is a poem that came out of this exercise by the young poet Kim Sais:

Jewels

Emeralds are eyes.
Rubys are roses.
Crystal is spring fresh.
Tulips are cups
Azalias are acribatic.
But silver is salty,
And gold is the world.
But I had to say goodbye,
And away I swirled.

Kim Sais

EXERCISE: Write a poem about animals.

One that is not "childish," since many of the greatest poets have become known for their poems on animals or fish. I am thinking specifically of Richard Eberhardt's beautiful poem "The Groundhog," which starts to be about a groundhog but leads to being a lament about the nature of death. One can write poems that begin as one thing and end as another—begin by talking about reality and end by being abstract.

EXERCISE: Write about gardens.

Stone gardens. English gardens. Gardens that I have seen in Zen temples. A way into the poem can often be choosing "key words" and writing them out. For example, if one writes about Zen gardens, one can choose the place names of the gardens and different aspects about them. Making a list of names first is often helpful. So that if I were writing about my time of living in Zen temples I might put down the following key words:

Daitokui Temples

Shuon-An Temples

Eastern Gardens

The Gate

Stone Pavement

The Abbot

The Reading Gate

The Inner Hall

Then with my "list" to go back to, the poem can proceed. Of course the more one creates poetry, the more all of this becomes second nature and the list is in the mind.

A large part of the joy of reading poetry is the escape that comes from trite forms. And a release for the ear and mind. By returning to the musicality of poetry (poetry came from incantation) one hears new sounds and new auditory measures. Poetry, if written not in "fancy" language (which is why so many people learn to hate poetry), is dead. We can expect from Chaucer beautiful old English—but wiring ourselves into the past is quite different from creating for the present. One of the great purposes of poetry is the freeing of conversation for its own melodies. That is the secret of T. S. Eliot, of Marianne Moore, of Elizabeth Bishop, and of William Carlos Williams. It is above all the secret I have not only tried to teach the young poets I work with but the secret I have learned from them.

The unconscious uses the artist as a medium through which it takes expression—the artist follows the creative influence and impulse, with a minimum of rational reference, allowing visions to crystallize.

What to write about?

Writing a poem FOR SOMEONE can be an exercise that is stimulating—the poem can be in the form of a "valentine." Here are two poems written by two of the young poets in my workshop:

A Valentine to Dorothy Hamill

Dear Dorothy Hamill,
I always dream about you.
You always comfort me when I watch you on T.V.
So let's give a cheer for Dorothy Hamill, my dear.
Happy Valentines Day to you and a happy "77" too.
From,
D
  O
    R
     I
       A
        N
         L
          A
           N
            G
             E

Love Is

Love is a scene bright
and warm Love is inside
in a cold snowy storm
Love is to see someone
you really like Love is
to hear soft music playing
just right Love is to
give things to people and
share but love to them

is to know that you care Love is to know
spring comes after
fall but love is to know
that you're loved and
that's best of all

Ariel Leve

To superimpose forms in a mechanical fashion (poetic forms) will create a craftsman—but not an artist. Those forms can be looked up in any traditional book on poetry and learned in one day. To be a competent craftsman is not what interests me as a poet. What does interest me is to trail my own self down to the end—to follow the streams of consciousness and use my poetry to emancipate me from the universe which is not totally "real" to me unless I join it with my own imaginary freedom and forces.

If a person has a native endowment—an ear that can hear, an eye that can see—he or she must add to that sensibility which is constantly being refined. What Laforgue calls "nerves" mixed with subconscious sensations and streams of consciousness can create a world of one's own. My last advice is that the manner of the poet should be as natural as possible and as unconstrained as possible. It should, at the same time, be subtle and wholly original.

Finally, a poet's mind should be free from any bias or convention. The approach to life should be direct and wholly personal. All the aesthetic doctrines, exercises, and precepts—whether they refer to technicalities of meter and rhythm, or wherever they "induce" a person to learn a lesson—are relative and liable to become a source of danger when insisted upon. To me "sloppy" writing is "stereotyped" writing rather than loose or amorphous writing. No clichés, no rhetoric, no metrical straightjacket—instead juxtaposition of seemingly disparate experiences—the "aesthetic" and the "colloquial"—it makes no difference if the word is "slang" or a "philosophical term."

Laforgue achieved in his work a kind of cosmic irony which cannot be imitated. He also kept a childlike innocence. We might do likewise. Laforgue did not hesitate to use everything he heard all around him as the words he threw into his poetry. Popular refrains, melancholy boisterous observations—all go into his work. I remember reading a quote from Laforgue which might serve as a way to end an unendable chapter—since

132

poetry is the impossible art. He wrote: "I am writing fanciful little poems which have only one aim. To be original at any cost." And in another letter: "Let us tell everything (after all, it is the squalor of life, more than anything else, which should impart to our lines a melancholy humor) but let us tell it in a subtle fashion."

Here are poems where I try to tell the impossible on the birth of my daughter:

The New Life

Night Swimming

I remember that slow island
Where you took me, once, in Asia
Where the crabs had great shields of thick light
And carried, on their backs, worlds of their own.
We copied them.
The phosphorescent water tucked us in
That ocean where we will not be again
And phosphorescent water held us down
Like two stars spinning, binaries that bobbed
Into the mangrove waves. Green
Diamonds cut our lips and we became
Constellations, partners near the moon.
Seaweed lit our nipples as we swam
Through silvery schools of fish. I
Did the dead man's float and then I called,
"Hurry. We must return!"

The Beginning

With my fingers
I design blue mosques and temples
On the linen, trace them
On the pillows
While my child

Puffs like a pillow in my flesh
And changes to a moonstone
Or a pearl. Tonight
My marrow flowers into coral.

And shall I dream, again, of minarets?
I live inside these temples
While the child
Grows in the great bulb of my shaking belly.
I see myself dance in the mirror's shards
Where life is ocean-heavy. Life begins—
Oh, dance with me until the ocean ends!
Once time and blood cells bobbed like barnacles
Scratching at my heels, until
I left those cords and bones. Now
Nothing's known.
Child,
Will you float my marrow to the world
And tell them who I am? Now you
Curve gently like a baroque pearl. And
As you swim through the yolk sac will you glide
Into this world of linen and new life?

The Eyes

Today your face
Grows rapidly.
Eyelid and
Ear shine
Under my skin
Like melons. We, roped
Together,
Float
In the universe
And one root

At a time, one
Vein at a time, we
Shift and I sleep
As your new eyes
Begin.

The Hands

White sprouts
Are opening. Are they
The new, soft hearts
Of peonies? ginger lilies?
Under my stone sea-snail
Belly, under that place
Of snow and sunlight,
Ivory anemones
Blow up inside me
And mushroom in the billows
Of my flesh. I ask myself
About the grace of fingers.
Fingernails,
Like bleeding hearts,
Grow under stones. I wake
And listen to what they
Have to tell me: "We are dumb
White flowers
Under the foreign side
Of the moon."

Love Song to the Unborn

Where the spinal cord gets hooked up to the past,
Where ancient loves
Get married, drowned, or lost,
I hook with the starfish.

Our joy is without spine. I rake
The faces out like clams
And wake, turning in pain.

Late summertime. My back
Is well again. How strange
Now to be able to lift things
Or open windows. I must unbend
And throw off blankets,
Unfold by the sea.

Now, by the beach, my toes
Are white roots inside water.
When it rains
I wait for the sun,
Snoozing inside the damp sheets
On this farm
When it is warm.

I lie on my back, flat on a pumpkin field,
My flesh puffed like a gourd,
The marigolds twined around my thighs.
Find me in the deep splash
Of pumpkins, squash,
And green leaves that prickle.
I rub my fingers on the skin
Of squash—skin white as papyrus,
Smoother than porcelain—
And look up at the sun.
I know that its strength will be your own.

Here tangled yellow flowers
Pinch like fingers.
You will be here next summer,
Singing of pumpkins in your ripe spine time.
Love, I take down this landscape in my mind.

Artaud said a poet must be like a person beckoning from the flames. It is important, for me, to write every day. As an exercise for the imagination, keeping sharp the senses the way a ballet dancer trains muscles. Talking about why he writes poetry, Stevens says, "A man doesn't spend his life doing this sort of thing unless doing it is something he needs to do."

What is the need of the poet? What *must* you say?

It is important to understand this—without this no one writes. What is the need?

If there is a need, and you can *center* on it, the poem will follow.

CHAPTER FOUR

Writing Songs

THE BEATLES WERE PUBLIC POETS. They were the first singings heralding a change in songwriting. They were not just popular mouthpieces for tin-pan alleys and chart songs—they were singing their own souls. They came along after Dylan Thomas died—and were popular while Sylvia Plath, Robert Lowell, Anne Sexton, and Ginsberg were being read on the college campuses. They too were confessional poets—and that was their appeal to young people. They were singing their own truths, their own words, their own rhythms, and appeal was basically in the lyrics, which they wrote themselves. They were a return to the singer as bard, the singer as historian, the singer as a commentator on ordinary feelings, and also the singer as a teller of secrets. The Beatles' songs—with lyrics by Paul McCartney and John Lennon—were a new beginning of the "unbanal" lyric. They were not in the "moon-spoon" business. They were in the business of writing poetry—of telling things about humanity in a rhythmical (rhyme) straight nonbullshit way. They were outgrowths of the lyricism of Dylan Thomas, the realism of John Osborne, and the experimentalism of the bardic French poets. The oddness and strangeness of "Le Bateau Ivre" of Rimbaud ("The Drunken Boat") was close to the almost surreal experimentalism of the lyrics and rhythms of the Beatles. They also expressed the loneliness and the need to communicate. People wanting to reach out to each other ("I Want to Hold Your Hand").

They were expressing—in songs and lyrics—two basic thoughts. One was the rejection of materialism and the normal social structure. The excitement of the Beatles, as in jazz, lay in the innocence and joy of unusual lyrics. The fifties had been a time of simple lyrics. Bill Haley and the Comets singing "Shake, Rattle and Roll" in 1954, Pat Boone singing "Ain't That a Shame!" and the Platters singing "Only You" in 1955, Presley singing "Hound Dog" and Fats Domino singing "Blueberry Hill" in 1956, Johnny Cash "I Walk the Line;" in 1957 Paul Anka singing "Diana," the Everly Brothers "Bye Bye Love," and Elvis Presley "All Shook Up!;" in 1958 Ricky Nelson singing "Poor Little Fool;" in 1959 the Platters singing "Smoke Gets in Your Eyes;" and in 1960 Chubby Checker "The Twist" and Elvis Presley "Stuck on You"—but suddenly we were in the sixties defined by our songs. "Let It Be" and "All My Loving" and "I Want to Hold Your Hand" sneaked up on the world not with a whimper—but a bang.

We were in the Beatles generation—a time when lyrics defined the life-style of a new generation, lyrics that fused blues, country and Western, rhythm and blues, and pure poetry. The lyric became more lyrical. And more mystical. By the time the Beatles broke up, the lyric had been influenced by poetry from the streets of Liverpool and mantras from the East. Rock, which had influenced the world with its loud, brash, crude rhythms and a beat that never stopped (from Alan Freed who first beat out rhythms with his fist on a telephone book) and also with its brash guitar and singing keyed toward ecstasy, was replaced by the new music of the Beatles which was more like Elizabethan poetry. The primeval subjects of rock and Little Richard's music were the shouted heavy vocals heavily based on blues and not concerned with complicated lyrics. Lyrically the Beatles' music was closer to poetry and changed the lyrics that were to come after it.

Songs are simplified poems.

For me "simplify" means writing lyrics which requires a scaling down of language but a stepping up of emotion. Lyrics are just another way of writing who you are and what you feel.

I first wrote songs because I met the outstanding composer Gary William Friedman, and I wanted to work with him. Together we wrote a musical called *Walking Papers*, which was done as a workshop in the fall of 1975 at the Circle in the Square in New York City. I realized while working with Gary how complicated the art of lyric writing was. But I also learned from Gary the fulfillment of working with another person.

After my first try at a play I met the composer Galt MacDermot. For him I wrote a new musical called *The Life Singer*—based on new awareness and also on the poem "The Love Singer."

Working with a talented composer is a blessing. I could never hope to write music as well as Gary Friedman or Galt MacDermot so I didn't even try. Let me tell you about Galt MacDermot and *The Life Singer*.

Writing lyrics is a way of heightening emotion and or reducing poems to simple themes. I connect "songs" and "poems" naturally since they both come out of content.

Hair with its innovative and historical tribal rock concept was a play that was almost all music, dance, and lyric. Two years ago I met the composer of this musical— Galt MacDermot. Before that, I had just seen his name on records. He was a "legend" for me as the composer of "Good Morning, Starshine" and "Age of Aquarius," both of which came out of *Hair*. I was putting together an evening of poetry that I had written as a scholarship evening for Bennington College and I asked Galt MacDermot if he would write or contribute some music. We met and began talking about poetry. Galt said he liked working with poets "because I love beautiful language in songs," and he sang for me some of the songs he had written for a production of *Troilus and Cressida* for Joseph Papp's Shakespearean theater. He asked me if I would like to create a play with him.

I wanted to work with Galt MacDermot and he was hoping that I would think of a poetic concept. I asked my friend Sybil Wong if she would help me create a story that would lend itself to poetic lyrics. We created the concept of the life singer.

The Life Singer is a play for the musical theater in which we try to capture an aspect of the seventies. As a poet I am trying to look into society and see what people are thinking, and how they are going about their lives. The key to the seventies, it seems to me, is meditation, change, growth, a new inner consciousness, body awareness, and a celebration of mind and body and spirit. It is not true for everyone of course. There are many who never change and cling to their odd and old lives and skin, but for others, especially the young, the term "new awareness" is not inappropriate.

My play is about the new awareness.

It is about the West being influenced by the strong power of the East. It takes seriously the wisdom that comes out of cosmic consciousness, but also has a sense of humor about it at the same time. The joke is that everyone is a guru! Each person his own life singer and his own poet.

I first made up the term "love singer" when I lived in Nepal and I saw, walking through the streets, a person who lived and looked like a mad person but was known to be a sage and poet. The man was treated with great respect and love, and instead of being laughed at for "not conforming" he was listened to and appreciated as a holy person. Although what he was saying I could not understand, I wrote a poem about him called "The Love Singer." This poem later became the basis for the musical.

The Life Singer is about a woman guru. She is sent by her mystical godmother to change the life of a loser called Richard. Through her understanding and sympathy Richard becomes a changed person. He is really enlightened; he uses his newfound psychic freedom to abuse her and has no appreciation for what her love has brought to him. Life Singer leaves Richard and goes on to make a life as a public figure enlightening masses of people. She misses Richard, gets tired of public life, and eventually goes back to him—giving her agent the role of the public guru. In the end her love for Richard changes him, and she is even more enlightened by her own humanity.

142

The Life Singer is about loneliness; it is partially autobiographical but in a less personal sense. The Life Singer is a poet, not me, but any artist, who tries to teach people how to look deep into themselves. The songs are often more lyrical and more abstract—although there are many book songs.

The first lyric written for Galt MacDermot was "The Song of the Outsiders." Richard is a dance teacher working at a dance studio, and his students are all of the lonely losers of the city who have no one to touch. They are reaching out and symbolize the alienation and isolation of individuals in an urban society. One of the requirements of this song was to write a lyric sung by a company—and also to define the company. The song has to tell who people on stage actually are. A song outside of a play can be a lyric that is apart—but here a song has to tell what is taking place on stage.

Song: "The Song of the Outsiders"

COMPANY

Who are we?
We're the people you never meet
We live in this city—dwarfed by bridges and towers

Who are we?
We're anonymous hands, faces and feet
We live in this city—we work and lose track of hours

We look for our own reflections in the city's wounds
Waiting and hoping for touch
We sweep our emotions clean under the new moon
Hoping to learn how to feel
Out of our nightmarish days we need something real

Who are we?
We're the people you never meet
We live in this city—dwarfed by time clocks and hours

After a day is done
We'd like to have some fun
Reach out and touch someone

After the sun goes down
We'd like to paint the town
But no one is around

Something exciting
Something inviting
Something romantic
Something unfrantic

Who are we?
We're the people you never meet
We live in this city—dwarfed by bridges and towers

Who are we?
We're strangers who search someone to touch
We live in the darkness—all of our most lonely hours

After a day is done
We'd like to have some fun
Reach out and touch someone . . .

EXERCISE: Write a lyric about being left out.

The lyric was set by Galt MacDermot to be almost like a ballad. The next lyric is another song defining Richard's role—but also can stand on its own. "Beginnings" can be the beginning of anything that is new.

Song: "Beginnings"
RICHARD

Beginnings
Everyone has their first time
To learn something
Everything has its beginnings

Don't be afraid
Everyone has to start somewhere

Don't be afraid
You'll look like a child but don't care

Don't be too frightened to let your big feet make a little flap
You'll be enlightened when you can move like that
    and like that and that

Don't be afraid
Everything has its beginnings

Don't be afraid
Soon you'll be movin' and swinging

You'll be delighted now that you've got a feather in your cap
You'll be excited to find that you're dancing tap
    on tap on tap on tap

Don't be afraid
Everyone must take a first step

Don't be afraid
There's best and better and best yet

Now you're expected to dance for the rest of your life like that
Once you're connected to your own partner dancing's just a snap

So dance
Lose yourself in a dance

Dance
That's what I'll give to you
Dance . . .

EXERCISE: Write a lyric about a first time.

The next lyric had the problem of presenting loneliness. Many of the thoughts were taken from my collected poems on loneliness. Especially the concept of looking at the ceiling. An exercise for writing lyrics might be to write a poem first (almost like an armature for a statue) and write a poem following it.

Song: "Hope It's Not Forever"

RICHARD

As you stare at the ceiling and the floor
And you wonder what you are living for
You hope it's not forever

When you're blue and you don't belong at all
There's no visitor, you know no one will call
You hope it's not forever

So you dream about a perfect human being
A wonder-person you have never seen
Who will not laugh at your dreams
Someone who is gentle and for real
Who will feel all the things that you feel

When you don't have anyone to care
And you have so much you want to share
You hope it's not forever

So you dream about a perfect human being
A wonder-person you have never seen

Who will not laugh at your dreams
Someone who is gentle and for real
Who will feel all the things that you feel

When you find yourself all alone at night
And you wonder if life will turn out right
You hope it's not forever
You hope it's not forever

EXERCISE: Write a song about time.

The oddest things can sometimes inspire lyrics. An example is the "Death Waltz" song. While I was writing this play Galt MacDermot had mentioned several directors that he admired, including Bob Fosse. "But I don't think this play will interest him" said Julie Arenal, who had choreographed *Hair*. "Why not?" "Because he almost died and he is making a film about death. I've heard that he is into everything about death." The idea came to me—why not write a death waltz? At least it will attract him to the play. After the lyric was written, I thought, "Even if Bob Fosse doesn't direct the play, I like the lyric." Several months later when we played the entire score for Bob Fosse I watched his face as he listened to "Death Waltz." I wondered if he had any idea that it was written just for him. But he listened the same way as he listened to the others—sensitively and impassively. He listened to them with the idea of "How many numbers can be choreographed?"—but, without knowing it, he was my muse.

Song:"Death Waltz"

OLD WOMAN

Fa da la da la la la
Life leads to nothing but death
Love leads to nothing but death
Everything leads to nothing but death
The question is——when?

A mere little germ
An accident, thrombosis, or attack

And suddenly you're dead
And that's that

Fa da la da la la la
Life leads to nothing but death
Love leads to nothing but death
Everything leads to nothing but death
The question is—when?

Death is my past time
But life is my profession
And so—since I must live
In order to die

At least I can think about death
And ask myself why?

Fa da la da la la la
Life leads to nothing but death
Love leads to nothing but death
Everything leads to nothing but death
The question is—when?

EXERCISE: Write a lyric about death or birth.

A lot of people write songs about poverty. One of my favorite songs is the lyric of Yip Harburg's "Brother, Can You Spare a Dime." For *The Life Singer* I wrote a song about wealth. It's an upside-down song—quite the opposite of "If I Had a Million" (lyrics by Will Holt). A good exercise for the subject of a song is to try writing a song about money.

Song: "I Hate Being Rich"

OLD WOMAN

What is it like to be rich?
Behind your back they call you son of a bitch

You meet all the big shots and brass
Who are such a pain in the ass

What is it like to be rich?
Between you and me I would much rather switch
With someone whose life is more plain
And money is not their sole aim

Who needs antiques?
Who needs a maid?
Who needs fur coats?
Who needs these horses?
Who needs boutiques?
Who needs this jade?
Who needs these boats?
Who needs divorces?

What is it like to be loaded?
In *Who's Who* and Dun and Bradstreet you're coded
Everyone wants contributions
For problems which have no solutions

Give to the sick
Give to the blacks
Give to the Jews
Give to the downtrodden
Give to the quick
Give to the quacks
Give to the muse
Something is rotten

What is it like to be rich?
You can't scratch your ass when you have an itch
What is it like to have money?
You never meet anyone funny

What is it like to be rich?
You ride your Rolls-Royce around town like a witch
What is it like to have money?
You're fucked but you're fucked over honey!

EXERCISE: Write a lyric about money.

Where does the subject of a song come from?

It can come from the same mysterious place that a poem comes from. From memory. Deep feeling. An article in a newspaper. A letter. A fantasy. A dream. An occasion. This song grew out of an article that I wrote for a magazine . . . a spoof on pornography. It was a satire of the exclusiveness of a whorehouse for men. I imagined a situation in reverse. Also I tried to capture a Brechtian cabaret quality. An exercise is: Write about sensuality. Poke fun at a serious subject. Here is "The House of Good Repute":

Song:"The House of Good Repute"

Richard and Male Whores

RICHARD
In the house of good repute
We'll have a lot of fun

In the house of good repute
We'll guarantee you'll come

What I'm gonna provide
Is really not complex
Come in and step inside
Into my house of sex

In the house of good repute
We'll have a lot of fun

In the house of good repute

We guarantee you'll come

Forget husbands and brats
Forget your household chores
You won't think of all that
You'll learn to love our whores

MALE WHORES

We're here to please you
We're here not to tease you
We're here to blow in your ears
Nice doctors and lawyers
We're not home destroyers
So don't you have any fears

TOGETHER

In the house of good repute
We'll have a lot of fun

In the house of good repute
We guarantee you'll come

MALE WHORES

We're here to stroke you
We're here not to soak you

We're here to get rid of your tears
Our professional manners
Will drive you bananas
You'll be contented my dears

TOGETHER

In the house of good repute
We'll have a lot of fun

In the house of good repute
We guarantee you'll come

EXERCISE: Write a lyric about sex. The end of a relationship.

The Country of the Hero" is a lyric closer than others to poetry. The concept here was to use language in an unusual way. "Walking in wishes" is a made-up grammatical line. Try writing a song in which there is a common subject talked about (here it is football) but it is a metaphor for something. "The Country of the Hero" is about power. One could write a song about the uselessness of power, but here I tried to say it in a way closer to the mystery of poetry and indirection rather than by saying exactly what I meant. An exercise: Write a lyric saying one thing but actually saying something else.

Song: "The Country of the Hero"

RICHARD

Walking in wishes and lovely for shame
I play the eternal hero's game
Venus lies star-struck asleep in soft sounds
The distance I cover is all green ground

What is it that makes me feel I am alive?
The country of the hero is the heart's size

Kick at the ball like the head of a god
Now dust and heaven beat under my heart
And as I run I can hear the crowds shout
Blood and my whole life I taste in my mouth

What is it that makes me feel I am alive?
The country of the hero is the heart's size

On the grass crowned by the wind of the east
I'm running like a child that's become a beast
And why do I soar to be such a hero?
Without the crowd I only feel sorrow

What is it that makes me feel I am alive?
The country of the hero is the heart's size

As I run with the ball crossing the goal
And I see that the world is a ball that I stole
As the crowd roars above the game and green
I'm a new hero but what does this mean?

What is it that makes me feel I am alive?
The country of the hero is the heart's size

EXERCISE: Write a lyric about a hero traveling.

Learn to Be Yourself" is a song about inner awareness. It tries to deal not with a story or a feeling but a philosophical idea—idea that all one wants is in the inner mind. An exercise for a lyricist is to write a lyric about an abstract thought.

Song: "Learn to Be Yourself"

LIFE SINGER

Don't tell me what you wish to be
Learn to be yourself and you'll be free

Don't tell me what you cannot be
Just find out what's inside
Don't try to change reality
Take what is real to be your guide

If you're soft——let yourself be that
Let yourself be called good
If you're lost——let yourself be that
Don't be false and you'll be understood

Don't tell me what you wish to be
Learn to be yourself and you'll be free

Don't tell me you can't get lovers
Find out what you can give
What count's not what's done by others
Through me you can learn a way to live

Don't tell me what you wish to be
Learn to be yourself and you'll be free

If you want to be smart you can be there
If you want to be still you can be that too
If you want to be a poet or a millionaire
Be yourself is all you have to do

Don't tell me what you wish to be
Learn to be yourself and you'll be free

EXERCISE: Write your own lyric about *change*. Changing your mind. Change in life.

Change" is a lyric that is an example of dramatic change in rhythm and length of stanza. It is a variation, as a lyric, and in musicality, on a song in which all the stanzas are metrically the same. The beginning of the song is personal observation. The middle of the song is general observation. And it goes back to the personal. The song itself changes not only rhythmically but psychologically from a personal observance of changes to a possibility of a change in the universe——from a mustard seed to the moon——an exercise that might come out of writing a song like "Change"——to take the same concept of a single idea to include taking a concept and looking at it from different ends of the looking glass——closely——and from an abstract distance. It doesn't have to be the concept of

"Change"—it could be Life, Death, Love, Habit, Birth, Rebirth—a universal idea looked at through different lenses of thought and intelligence.

Song: "Change"

Dolores and Richard

DOLORES

Change——I can see hat you've changec
    ——I can see you are not the person you used to be
Change——I can see that you've changed
    ——I can see that you're someone who might be for me

Change——I can see that you've changed
    ——I can see in your body and in your complexion
Change——There's a newness not the same
    ——Suddenly everything's new in my affection

TOGETHER

Change is like the sun
Change touches everyone
The sea can change
The rain can change
And change is never done

Change is all we know
Change turns the sun to snow
The moon can change
The cloud can change
And change is all we know

DOLORES

Change——I can see that you've changed
        ——I can see you are not the person you used to be
Change——I can see that you've changed
        ——I can see that you're someone who might be for me

One of the first virtues of a poet writing lyrics, Galt made me realize, is that poets, like schizophrenics or comedians, think in odd connections. "I have trailed love down to the end" is an example of the odd connection between trailing love to the end of its path and trailing a piece of thread to the end of its spool——thus the word "embroidery" weaves into a pattern odd connections made only by a stream-of-consciousness connection. This song came from a poem.

An unusual use of words is here and is put into a song.

Song: "I Have Trailed Love Down to the End"

LIFE SINGER

I have trailed love down
To the end

And under the sun
I have heard what the ear refused
What the eye could not see
What the mind takes down at night like embroidery

In a sense, I have seen myself
Have sewn up his grief

And then?
Oh, our love was so brief

I have trailed love down
To the end
And under the sun
I was really very amused

For all that I could see
Was the newness of life I had all around me

In a sense, I have seen myself
Have sewn up his grief

And then?
Oh, our love was so brief

EXERCISE: Write a lyric on the theme of love ending.

Another song based on a poem is "The Life Singer"——which became the title of the play. The job of this song was to expand the original poem to include all of the ideas in this play.

Song: "The Life Singer"

RICHARD

Suddenly she appeared
Looking quite mad and weird
Talking a language I didn't understand
Her eyes were gay and she seemed to have sight
About the world and how to make things right

And I said to myself
That's the Life Singer
I said to myself
That's the Life Singer

She spoke in a new way
Of love and work and play
Talking a language I didn't understand
Her goodness seemed out of her face to shine
I drank her words up as if they were wine

And I said to myself
That's the Life Singer
I said to myself
That's the Life Singer

She held her hand in mine
Existing out of time
Talking a language I didn't understand
Never did I talk ever so softly
Never did I walk ever so surely

And I said to myself
That's the Life Singer
I said to myself
That's the Life Singer

EXERCISE: Write a lyric about a strange person.

There are many other songs in the play and some of the lyrics are here:

Song: "I'm Gonna Devote My Life to Pushing You"

AGENT
I
'm tired of Barbra Streisand
I'm tired of Erica Jong
I'm tired of Frank Sinatra
I'm tired of kissing King Kong

I'm tired of pushing big talents who always make me feel blue
I'm gonna devote my life to pushing you
I'm tired of corporate products
And wasting my talents on crap
I'm tired of dealing with odd ducks
And putting their names on the map

I'm tired of all these people telling me what I ought to do
I'm gonna devote my life to pushing you

I always knew a madonna
Would come into my life
And she'd mean more than my mother or my mistress or my wife
She'd tell the world a way to find itself and be aware
And I'll make sure that seats are sold
And everyone is there

I'm gonna devote my life to pushing you . . .

EXERCISE: Write a lyric that makes fun out of a profession. The song can be funny or political.

Song: "One Morning You'll Wake Up and Enter Life"

COMPANY

One morning you'll wake up and enter life
You'll run quite swiftly through the mountains
Passing the palm trees and civets
Watching harvests and children
All in the ripeness of summer
It is then you've inherited joy
The way one inherits a fortune

One morning you'll wake up and enter life
You'll have gone beyond a place you knew
Passing your face in the mirror
You'll be your cosmic child
Catching white birds in the sunshine
It is then you've inherited joy
The way one inherits a fortune
One morning you'll wake up and enter life . . .

EXERCISE: Write a lyric about a vision.

Song:"Hello Again"

RICHARD

Hello again, loneliness
She made me feel so good
Hello again, loneliness
Amazingly I was understood

She knew me
My shoes, my moods, my dreams, my life-mistakes
She knew me
My lies, my fears, my schemes, my rotten breaks
I want her back
That's all I know
It's too late for that
She melted like the snow

Hello again, loneliness
She made me feel so sane
Hello again, loneliness
Suddenly I was a child again

All I have felt
Is a memory of her
That will never end

Hello again
Loneliness, my friend

EXERCISE: Write a lyric about isolation.

Song:"Get Her by Any Mean Necessary"

OLD WOMAN

Now first you must find out
What makes her smile—or pout
Then find out where she's living
What she needs and start giving

Get her by any mean necessary

Then you must ascertain
What pleases her again
If she say no convert her
And swear you never hurt her

Get her by any mean necessary

If she's political
You be political
If she's a Buddhist
You be a Buddhist
If she's into beans and rice
You claim health foods very nice
If she likes sports
You hire a tennis court
If she's into psychoanalysis
You discuss your ego paralysis
If she wants to be a wife
You put a ring on her for life
Get her by any mean necessary

Go after her
Go after her
Woo her
Screw her
Say you never leave her

Get her by any mean necessary

EXERCISE: Write a lyric about getting what you want.

Song:"Illuminations"

COMPANY

And then? Colors and names of colors
Colors are lights that make us come alive
And then? Colors and names of colors
Illuminated by our own light we have nothing now. We have to hide

Colors shine from our body, from arms, feet, legs and face
Colors project our aura into our own inner space

Colors are our language
How shall we begin?
We were not shown a way
To speak of pain when we were young
Although we listened to the lizard's tongue
And heard the stars lamenting as they glide
Into the foaming zodiacs to hide
And we conceived celestial things as having different colors
Each animal and bird and mineral has its own color
And halos break inside of us in hues of pain and joy

Colors, halo colors
Auras bleeding purple bleeding pink
Colors, cosmic colors
Running through the life-lines of our veins
Coloring the life-maps of our minds
Colors are medications for our time . . .

   (Speak)

Colors. We live our life out in illuminations
And sometimes we are not even aware of these auras
These lights around our body that we sometimes cannot see.

EXERCISE: Write a lyric about what you see.

My feeling about writing lyrics is that the process is not as mysterious as people. To write a lyric there is no "secret" except for the secret of one's thoughts. Dick Shawn, talking about comedy, defines the art of the comedian as "talent plus control." The lyric takes sensitivity but the control is the technique of following a rhyme pattern—which anyone can do once there is a model. The real lyric, the real song, comes out of your guts and your need to either say something or accommodate the song to a character through whose mind one is speaking.

In writing songs, as in writing poems, the main thrust is to have courage and not need constant approval. The ability to make mistakes and to go on is simply learning the writing process. Writing is never boring. It is a way of life. A way to keep renewing the self. Most children are not afraid—that is why they are natural poets or natural lyricists. They are directly connected to their unconscious. The streams of imagination are always flowing and there is no real voice inside of them to say, "No, you cannot say that." The older we are, the harder it is to take risks.

But writing is risking everything. Telling about one's life. Daring to be foolish. Making a fool of oneself and not being afraid of someone laughing at you. The true writer is the life comedian.

Later, in college, I began to write literary poems. I was taught the poems of Lowell and Marianne Moore and I tried to write in ways like them. I was, in my own way, finding "my own voice."

I found that "my own voice" was daring to write about my own experiences. If all I knew about was childhood, then I would write about childhood. I found "my voice in poetry" quite early by writing about what I knew. And so when I teach young people, I say quite honestly that one cannot teach poems; one can only encourage oneself—or others—to write about what they know, what they have experienced or thought or imagined.

I use myself in poems as my own instrument. It is only by experience—by life experience—that I have grown as an artist. By lovely experiences that have brought out the celebration in me.

I would say that going to boarding school (the Cherry Lawn School) was important to me. At eight I had an unusual teacher who exposed children to Shakespeare and T. S. Eliot. From the poetry of T. S. Eliot I learned the importance of "conversation" in verse. In high school I appeared in many poetic plays—by Lorca, by Eliot, by Shakespeare. I began studying in high school the theories as well as the poetry of Eliot. From T. S. Eliot I learned the importance of colloquial speech. How he, like Shakespeare and Marlowe, was able to move me to "want to be a writer."

Even as a child I wanted to write. To make something "come alive" with words. The excitement that I felt when I first saw poems "published" in the yearbook—and later my first "published poem" in a magazine—there are no words to express my feelings. Suddenly I felt that I had some permanence—some stake in history. I often think that the "need to write" is very close to the "need for roots." Certainly I was a child from a divorced home. I was literally "homeless." It was writing that gave me a home. I lived inside my imagination and inside the paper that I wrote my dreams down on. I made poems good enough to "live in." So it seems that writing is "where I live." I live in my poems.

Wiring music into myself, I had my "special" poets who became my friends. My own poems became like friends to me also. A way of befriending myself. Most of all I appreciated, in boarding school, T. S. Eliot. He was so critical of the modern world. And reflected my own despair with the world of technology. Is that all there is? he asked. "Birth, copulation, and death?" Since I was seeking my own self, this poem reflected my own thoughts. I learned that a great poem is one in which others mysteriously see all their own life-secrets reflected.

Life experience is everything in writing for a poet. Of course one may "imitate" any of the masters—but ultimately it is the self one comes back to. I remember my teacher, Howard Nemerov, saying to me in college, "It all begins in the home." That was, for me, the most important lesson I ever learned from someone else. He was giving me "permission" to write about the things that troubled me, since I had no

164

"home" but rather several "homes" (as a child I lived in boarding school with all the other misfits and orphans). My home was my grandparents' house, my father's hotel room, or my mother's small apartment where her three children from her second marriage and her husband and mother-in-law all lived in a crowded space of four rooms. The three children lived in one bedroom. She and her husband in another. And her mother-in-law slept in the living room. That meant there was no "home" for me. No bed for me. No closet for me. I felt like a bird deprived of a motherly nest.

Likewise my father had no "home" for me. He lived in a hotel room—a one-room studio apartment with a Murphy bed. There was no bed for me there either. My grandparents lived in an enormous apartment on West End Avenue, but even there there was no room for me. All of the rooms "belonged" to my mother's sisters and brothers. I "shared" a room with the maid. I used the bed on vacations and she stayed there when I wasn't there. It was her clothes in the closet—and so, apart from boarding school, all of my young life I was homeless. The only trouble with boarding school was that it was so transient One year you slept in a double-decker in Stein House. Another year you slept in the Manor House. You were always changing rooms, houses, roommates. But at least the territory was the same. Still—I felt homeless all through childhood and girlhood. After my parents' divorce when I was seven, I had no place of my own ever again until I grew up and had my own apartment. This search for "permanence" and "territory" led me as a child to withdraw and write poems. I could at least "save" the poems and take them with me. They were my portable life. My portable Me.

The portable Me was always comic.

I found that it was "okay" to be funny in poems. I learned that from T. S. Eliot. He was funny. He was satiric. He was romantic. His poems could be spoken. They were real. I felt as if they were about magic, loneliness, old age (who but a child understands so well about old age?), and also about modern man's alienation. In that sense, as an alienated child I understood "modern man's condition." Not from T. S. Eliot. But from my own life. I connected my own fears, my own life, my own unhappiness to him.

Unhappiness is the greatest teacher for a poet. I learned from my homelessness and aloneness what "feeling bad" means. I felt deeply. My aloneness was a wound. The great thing about the life of a poet—of any artist really—is that sadness is the great teacher. Sadness. Plus observance. Plus the ear that truly hears. The ear that does not hear—the eye that does not see—this is the person who will never learn how to write poems or songs. Life is the secret. And opening oneself up to one's life—the truth of it, the difficulty of it—prepares one for the life song.

CPSIA information can be obtained
at www.ICGtesting.com
Printed in the USA
BVOW04s0205120417
480933BV00006BA/78/P